What People Are Saying About Succeeding in College and Life

"Wong delivers a practical guide for students in how to survive and thrive during the college experience and beyond."

— Julia Keiko Matsui Estrella, Author of *Being Local in Hawai'i*

"Appropriate for everyone, Wong shows that you can succeed in college no matter your age or position in life, whether you're just out of high school or a working professional needing to go back for more or to start over."

— Doris Chu, M.A., Author of *Agent of God: Helping Your Family Survive Upcoming Disasters*

"Great information and stories! Through his own experiences and those of his students, Wong shows, at a deeply personal level, what it takes to make it through college and in life."

— Kapono R. Kobylanski, MBA, Author of *Waking Up: With No Excuses*

"Very inspiring. The lessons learned here are applicable not just to college, but to life itself."

— Jeffery Bow, Author of *Stop Thinking, Start Believing: How to Break Through Fear and Ignite Your Brilliance*

"Funny, witty, and charming. Wong's personal take on the college experience both as a student and instructor connects on all levels."

— Emmy-Lea Agustin, MS, CCLS, Author of
Becoming a Professional Role Model

"Very personable read. The personal stories Wong shares of both himself and students he's worked with over the years shows that you can succeed in college no matter your age or background."

— Karen "Lucky" Thornton, CEO Quantum Institute International, Author of *Transforming Mind to Matter*

"Wong provides practical advice that's applicable not only in college but in all stages of your life. College success skills are definitely life success skills."

— Susan Ortolano, MA, PCC, Intuitive Relationship, Marriage Coach, and Author of *Remarrying Right*

"For those who want a comprehensive approach to maximizing their college experience, you can't find a better guide than *Succeeding in College and Life*. You'll not only succeed; you will excel!"

— Meredith Herrenbruck, Author of
Becoming Ridiculously Awesome

"This is more than a college success book. It's a life success book."

— Heather Howell, Author of *Dream It, See It, Believe It*

"Jam-packed with a wealth of solid, practical, and easy-to-implement advice, this book is a 'must read' for everyone seriously interested in succeeding in college and in life."

— Susan Friedmann, CSP, International Bestselling Author of *Riches in Niches: How to Make it BIG in a small Market*

"As an ethnic minority, Wong provides a great road map and example for other students of color to succeed not only in college but in life as well."

— Laurie Nichols Bethell, Minister, Holistic Health Practitioner, Certified Transformational Breath Practitioner, and Author

"Where was this book when I was going through college?"

— Natalie Kawai, Author of *Conversations with Mother Goddess*

"As a former college instructor, I wish I could have given a copy of this book to every single one of my freshman composition students. It contains every tool a student needs to succeed, from time-management and study skills to dealing with being away from home for the first time and staying ahead of the game in preparing to enter the job market. It's the perfect graduation gift for high school students."

— Tyler R. Tichelaar, Ph.D. and Award-Winning Author of *Narrow Lives* and *The Best Place*

SUCCEEDING IN COLLEGE AND LIFE

HOW TO ACHIEVE YOUR
GOALS AND
LIVE YOUR DREAMS

JONATHAN WONG, MBA, M.ED, MPA

AVIVA
PUBLISHING
New York

**Succeeding in College and Life:
How To Achieve Your Career Goals and Live Your Dreams**

Copyright © 2017 by Jonathan Wong

All Rights Reserved. No part of this book may be used or reproduced in any manner whatsoever without the expressed written consent of the author, except in the case of brief quotations with credit embodied in articles, books, and reviews.

Address all inquiries to:
Jonathan Wong
P.O. Box 23259
Honolulu, HI 96823
(213) 262-9570
www.SucceedinginCollegeandLife.com

ISBN: 978-1-9431643-0-1
Library of Congress Control Number: 2015946506

Editor: Tyler Tichelaar, Superior Book Productions
Cover and Interior Design: Nicole Gabriel, AngelDog Productions

Published by:

Aviva Publishing
Lake Placid, NY
(518) 523-1320
www.avivapubs.com

Every attempt has been made to source properly all quotes.

Printed in the USA
First Edition

For additional copies visit:
www.SucceedinginCollegeandLife.com

Disclaimer

The material provided in this book is for informational purposes only and not for the purpose of academic advice. Use of this book and the materials contained within do not create an advisor-client relationship between Jonathan Wong, The Pono Way, LLC, and the reader. The opinions expressed herein are the opinions of the individual author. Any academic decisions you make are yours and yours alone, and you bear the ultimate responsibility for any results that may occur. There are many life conditions and factors that affect your chance for academic success and graduation, including but not limited to life events such as sudden long-term illness, family obligations, relationship issues, the academic rigor of your courses, instructional quality, and financial difficulties. You understand that Jonathan Wong and the The Pono Way, LLC do *not* guarantee that you will pass your courses or graduate as a result of your use of the information in this book. Jonathan Wong or the The Pono Way, LLC is not liable for any losses or perceived losses you may incur.

DEDICATION

This book is dedicated to all the awesome professors I had the privilege of studying with and under through the years.

- The liberal arts faculty of Honolulu Community College
- The faculty of the School of Communication at the University of Hawaii at Manoa
- The Information Systems faculty of Hawaii Pacific University
- The Information Technology faculty of the University of Phoenix, Hawaii Campus
- The instructors of the Hawaii Technology Institute
- The MBA faculty at the Shidler College of Business
- The faculty of the Education Technology and Education Administration departments at the University of Hawaii at Manoa, College of Education
- The faculty of the Public Administration and Peace Studies departments at the University of Hawaii at Manoa, College of Social Sciences

So many hours, so many people, so many lessons. But they've all stuck with me throughout the years and provided the foundation for the successful career and the successful business I've been able to build for myself and the lives I've been able to impact through my work. I have been truly blessed throughout my life to have studied with some of the greatest, most brilliant minds in the world in so many fields of study. Thank you for all your knowledge and nurturing. I hope I have honored your teachings with the work I have done throughout my career.

To my former colleagues at the University of Hawaii, especially my colleagues at Honolulu and Kapiolani, it was an honor to work alongside you all those years day in and day out in the trenches. It was through your example each and every day that I honed and grew as a teacher, advisor, support professional, and into the leader that I am today.

To all my colleagues at Kapiolani who worked with me on the MyPlan project which provided the framework for this text. It was a privilege and honor to work on such a forward-thinking, holistic, and comprehensive project with you.

To my ex-wife and college sweetheart, Shelley, for being there beside me through our journey as undergrads, graduate students, and working professionals for all those many years we walked the path of life together.

To our nephew Jacob who begins his collegiate journey very soon, Uncle loves you and is very proud of the man you've grown to become. Enjoy your college years. You just may meet someone special who will change your life forever.

To my parents, Allen and Charlotte Wong. You'll always be the first and greatest teachers of my life, and I am forever indebted to your sacrifices on my behalf.

To my brother, Mike, and sister-in-law, Maureen, for always supporting me through the darkest times in my life.

And to my beloved Liane. Thank you for supporting my dreams and giving me the freedom to grow my business and build our future and for believing in me when it felt like no one else did—including myself. I love you more than you'll ever know.

ACKNOWLEDGMENTS

A big mahalo (thank you) to the following individuals without whom this book would not have been possible.

To Patrick Snow, the greatest book publishing and marketing coach on the planet, who taught me and helped me realize my dreams of becoming a published author.

To Nicole Gabriel for the most beautiful book covers on the planet.

To Tyler Tichelaar, who makes my writing sound far more sophisticated and technically masterful.

To Brodi Goshi, Sunny-Aloha Miller, Justine Gronwald, Jodi Uehara, and John Noland, who helped support and promote me at the launch of my venture.

CONTENTS

Introduction	17

PART I: THE COLLEGE JUMPSTART

Chapter 1: Choosing a Career	25
Chapter 2: Picking Your Major	37
Chapter 3: Selecting the Right School	47
Chapter 4: Developing Your Academic Plan and Picking Your Classes	57
Chapter 5: Financing Your College Education	67
Chapter 6: Using Campus Resources—Building Your Support Team	85
Chapter 7: Getting Involved on Campus—Making the Most of Your College Experience	113

PART II: COLLEGE SKILLS FOR SUCCESS

Chapter 8: Making Friends—The Power of Study Groups	133
Chapter 9: Managing Your Time—So Much to Do, So Little Time	139
Chapter 10: Knowing Your Learning Style—The Best Way for You to Learn	151

Chapter 11: Reading for Efficiency—So Much Reading, So Little Time   157

Chapter 12: Improving Your Writing—Proper Written Communication   161

Chapter 13: Taking Good Notes—Recording What You're Hearing   169

Chapter 14: Processing Information with Mind and Concept Maps—Visualizing Concept Relationships   175

Chapter 15: Making Study Aids—Tools to Succeed   181

Chapter 16: Preparing for Tests and Exams—Are You Ready?   189

Chapter 17: Brainstorming—Unlocking Your Mind   195

Chapter 18: Overcoming Writer's Block—Words Just Don't Come Easy   199

Chapter 19: Picking Research Topics—Because You Need To   205

Chapter 20: Avoiding Plagiarism—Giving Credit Where It's Due   211

Chapter 21: Leveraging Technology—Make Technology Work for You   217

PART III: PEOPLE SKILLS

Chapter 22: Building Relationships with Your Instructors   231

Chapter 23: Building Relationships with Your Classmates—Lifetime Colleagues and Friends — 241

PART IV: MONEY MANAGEMENT AS A STUDENT

Chapter 24: Living on a Student Budget—Developing Healthy Money Habits — 249

Chapter 25: Money Saving and Money-Making Hacks for the College Student — 259

PART V: FORTITUDE FOR SUCCESS

Chapter 26: Mastering Your Emotions—Emotional Intelligence — 275

Chapter 27: Managing Your Stress—It's a Killer — 297

Chapter 28: Building Your Support Network—They've Got Your Back — 315

Chapter 29: Asking for Help Is Okay—It's the Smart Thing to Do — 323

Chapter 30: Failing Is Okay—You Can't Win Them All — 331

Chapter 31: Maintaining a Balanced Life as a Student—a Juggling Act — 339

Chapter 32: Nurturing Your Faith and Spirit—Connecting with Source — 349

— 359

PART VI: FROM COLLEGE TO CAREER

Chapter 33: Developing Your Practical Career Skills While a Student — 359

Chapter 34: Finding a Post-College Job While a Student—Making Your Next Move — 369

A Final Word...Achieving Your Destiny — 385

About the Author — 389

Pono Life Coaching — 391

Akamai Visionary Consulting — 393

Jonathan Speaks — 395

Drive for Uber or Lyft — 397

INTRODUCTION

"Every beginner possesses a great potential to be an expert in his or her chosen field."

— Lailah Gifty Akita, *Think Great: Be Great!*

Graduating from college is still a privilege that is fairly exclusive in nature. Statistics published in a 2013 study show that only 59 percent of students who begin a college degree wind up finishing within six years. If you are college bound, which side of this statistic do you want to be on? The 59 percent who graduate? Or the 41 percent who do not? Are you prepared for success? College is a rite of passage in life that most of us are expected to tackle. It is usually a critical transition time in our lives when we leave the comfort and safety of our parents' care and blossom into adulthood, finding ourselves and setting the course for our adult lives. Like any other testing point in our lives, though, there are many fears, questions, and anxieties we may face.

If you're just out of high school, some of the questions you may be asking yourself are: Am I ready for college? Can I handle college level work? Am I ready to be responsible for myself? Am I ready to live out of my parents' shadow? Can I balance the responsibilities of going to school, doing my homework, and doing it well while holding down a job to pay my own bills? Can I overcome the temptation to skip class and party? Can I live away from home without my family and friends there to support me? Is college really for me? College is so expensive! How will I be able to afford it?

Or perhaps you're a little bit older and are returning to school after many years. Some questions going through your mind might be: Do I have it in me to do schoolwork again? Am I too old for this? Can I handle going to school while holding down my job and supporting my family? How will I be able to afford school? I haven't had to do math since I was a kid, so how will I do it now?

These feelings and fears are very natural and valid. I've been there myself! Over the course of my undergraduate and graduate school career, I asked myself these questions hundreds of times. I was in college for the better part of seventeen years between my high school graduation in 1996 and the time I completed my last graduate degree in 2013. Through those years, I juggled the responsibilities of a college student with a career, raising a family, and all the challenges in between. We are all human and all struggle with many of the similar challenges that get in our way of succeeding in our studies. Maybe you're entering school or moving on to higher classes without a firm grasp of key concepts that cause you to struggle. Maybe you are battling a chronic and long-term illness that forces you to stay on the sidelines. Perhaps you are facing lots of challenges at home, such as domestic violence or other relationship issues. Or perhaps you struggle with keeping a roof over your head and are constantly moving, trying to cope with a lack of stability in your life. Through my schooling, I faced all of these challenges.

In this book, I will share with you many of the tips, tools, and secrets I have used personally and have taught to hundreds of students over the past fourteen years during my time as a college success instructor. Some of the topics we'll cover in this book include:

- finding the right career path and major for you
- finding the right school
- choosing the right classes
- funding your college education
- tips for studying, note-taking, reading, writing, and conducting research
- managing your time
- leveraging technology
- managing your money as a college student
- networking and building relationships with your classmates and instructors
- planning for and launching your career as a college student

Beyond college, though, I also want to set you up for life success! The skills you need to achieve college success are also, at the end of the day, life success skills. Nowadays, it is not uncommon for people to question the value of a college education. Make no mistake about it—the skills you learn in college, both in and out of the classroom, will serve you throughout your career and in your everyday life. In this book, I will share how everything we learn translates back to your life outside the classroom in your career and your daily life.

During my seventeen years in school, I earned an AA degree (1998), a BA degree (1999), an MBA degree (2007), an M.Ed degree (2010), and an MPA (2013). Through those years, I faced my share of challenges: chronic illnesses and hospitalizations;

moving homes several times, including bouts of couch surfing with family and friends between finding more permanent homes; raising my family; a period of separation in my marriage; a demanding career that I had to put ahead of my studies at times to my academic detriment; financial struggles; and caring for my elderly mother and coping with her eventual death. Earning my degrees did not come easy, especially as time went along and I faced more responsibilities. There were periods in my degree work when I was forced to drop grades or repeat courses because I either had to drop out or take F grades or Incompletes due to challenges occurring in my personal or professional life. Those times forced me to reevaluate my life, come to terms with my limits, and realize that sometimes it is not possible to do everything at once, so I had to prioritize what needed to be done. Sometimes, I needed to put my family needs ahead of school and step back. Sometimes, I needed to put my job ahead of my school and step back. During times of illness, I had to take care of myself first and foremost and put school on the back burner. Despite all the times school was set aside, however, the key was always coming back, picking up the ball, and finishing what I had started.

My college success story is not unlike the stories of thousands of students who came before me, and it won't be unlike your own story if you make the commitment to start and see your education through. Your dreams of finishing college are achievable, and I want to help you achieve them so you can build the best life possible for you and your loved ones.

I want to be your coach, your mentor, and your accountability partner! Just as it takes a village to raise a child, so it takes a strong support system to get you through school or any other difficult or challenging endeavor. I invite you to include me in your support network as you begin your college journey. I will share with you all the tools, tips, and techniques I used to complete five college degrees over the course of seventeen years. I have shared these stories with thousands of students during the last fifteen years through various workshops and classes that enabled them to fulfill their college dreams. I will never claim to know all the answers, but I will share with you everything that I know works.

With all of that said, are you ready to set yourself up for college and life success? Are you ready to tackle college head-on, prepare for your future, and build the life you've always dreamed of? Are you ready to learn about yourself and your place in the world? If so, let's get started!

To your college and life success!

With aloha, your friend,

Jonathan K Wong

Jonathan Wong, MBA, M.Ed, MPA

Honolulu, Hawaii

PART I
THE COLLEGE JUMPSTART

1

CHOOSING A CAREER

"Choose a job you love and you will never have to work a day in your life."

— Confucius

A Look Ahead...

In this chapter, we will explore the need to consider your career direction. Most folks go to college to learn a skill so they can get a good job to make good money. Identifying your career direction, therefore, is important prior to or early in your college career. Your career direction will help to define which academic major you should select to give you the tools you'll need for your chosen career field.

Everyone is different, so everyone is at a different point in his or her life journey when starting college. Perhaps you have always known the general direction you want your life to take; you have a good idea what you "want to be when you grow up." If so, that's awesome!

But perhaps you're not quite too sure what it is you "want to be when you grow up," so you may need to spend some time exploring your interests and values and inventorying your skills to come up with viable career options. That's okay, too.

Or perhaps you are returning to school after being in the workforce or attending to other life priorities such as raising a family or caring for elderly or ill family members. You are at a point in your life when you need a life change, and you want to explore a new vocation or progress further in your current vocation through skills updating. All of this is fine. We each go to school for our own unique reasons specific to us. Life is not a competition. We are all on our own unique journeys, so it's important not to judge or compare yourself to others.

Here are some quick stories from myself and others who had to find their career directions or reinvent their careers when they started college.

A General Direction Helps

I have always been fascinated with the media. Growing up in the '80s and '90s, I listened to the radio; played video games on my Atari and Nintendo; and watched Saturday morning cartoons, TV sitcoms, and Hollywood blockbuster movies. I was a media addict. As such, I knew I wanted some type of career in the media industry. I thought about being a radio DJ, working for the local TV station, being employed by a film production company or Hollywood studio, or working for a video game developer. I couldn't quite decide exactly what it was I wanted to do, but I knew I wanted to work *somewhere* in the wide field of media, communications, or entertainment. By the time I was finishing high school and evaluating colleges, I knew I wanted to major in something that would help me launch a career somewhere in the media field. I'll save that story for the next chapter, though.

Sometimes Directions Change

During my undergrad years, I had a friend who had entered college with a solid career goal. She wanted to be a successful businesswoman in the technology sector. Her motivation for this career field? She wanted to make good money. What better way to make money than studying business and working in the technology field? Can't beat the logic there.

But sometimes the goals you set for yourself aren't the right ones for you. You'll know that when things just aren't working out the way you want. She struggled through her accounting, finance, and programming classes. She didn't have the skills or interest to work with numbers; consequently, her grades suffered. She eventually realized the business and technology career path wasn't right for her, so she knew she needed to make a change.

By nature, she was a helping person, not a number cruncher. After a ton of soul searching, she decided she wanted to go into a helping profession—like social work or something in the social services. We will pick up her story in Chapter 2.

College Will Help You Reach Your Career Goals, No Matter Who or Where You Are in Life

The great thing about college and education is that it is always there, and it is accessible to everyone, no matter how old you are or where you are at in your life. It's a lot like church in that sense.

College takes all comers, no matter what.

For example, I have earned three master's degrees. I made the conscious decision to go back to school over and over again because college offered me certain tools I needed at different times as my career goals changed.

After I finished my bachelor's degree, I was lucky enough to get a job overseeing math tutoring at the local community college I'd attended and worked at throughout my undergraduate years. It wasn't something I saw myself doing or being qualified to do forever, so I knew coming in that it was only a temporary gig. I was job searching throughout that process, but my job searches were futile. Even with my bachelor's degree, I did not have the skills people were looking for. I knew I had to go back for more training.

My goal then was to get into the technology field. I always loved technology. I was good at it, and it paid good money—*really* good money. So I decided I wanted to be a certified IT professional. I would spend the next year attending classes and being trained as an IT professional through three different schools and programs.

Upon completion of my technician training, I did land a better paying and more stable job as a tech at the same college where I worked. I pursued that career for a good two years and had fun. But I realized that I wanted more out of life than just being a "tech guy." At the time, my job wasn't fully secure because it was grant-funded and I only had a three-year contract. I wasn't sure whether I would stay with the college as a career, and I had a lot of other ambitions. I had always dreamed of owning my own business or various businesses, so I decided to attend business school.

A few years went by, and as I was completing business school, my career at the college took off. With my graduate degree, I was offered more advancement opportunities. My employers started to invest in me based on the work and value I brought to the table from the skills I'd developed in my graduate work. At that point, I fell in love with my university career and decided to go "all-in" with it. I was done with my business degree by then, but since I intended to make education my career, I knew I needed to be more credentialed, so I wound up getting an education degree.

Several years later, I had finished my training in education, advanced in my career, and received a sizable promotion. At this stage, I decided to earn an additional degree to set up my future for more advanced possibilities in the university or at a high level within the government sector.

Each and every time I went back to school, it was with purpose and a specific goal in mind. Each degree led to increased career advancement and possibilities. Education is always a good investment—it is an investment in yourself.

Know and Find Thyself

Life is a continuous journey. As you can see both through my story and the story of my undergrad friend, our career paths and goals evolved as we experienced life and learned more about ourselves, our wants, our desires, and our skills. I entered college with a general idea of what I wanted. As I progressed through life, my goals and dreams changed, so I needed to learn different skills to get what I wanted. Many people choose to come back to school later in life during their careers to learn new skills, upgrade old skills, or make career changes.

My friend entered college with a career goal that she came to realize wasn't the right one for her. So she made a change midway through college and got on the right path for her. That is fine, too. Many students change their goals and majors several times during their college careers. Ideally, though, you'll want to do self-exploration work upfront so you can find the right path for you early and not have to learn things the harder way.

During my time as a student success instructor at community colleges, I worked with hundreds of students each semester to help each one *find* him- or herself and evaluate career goals. The students I worked with are a cross section of the human race:

- Students just out of high school who knew exactly what they wanted
- Students just out of high school with no clue what they wanted to do
- Students returning to school after either losing their careers or deciding they needed a career change
- Students returning to school after years of being parents or caregivers of a loved one
- Students returning to school after being released from prison
- Students returning to school to retrain or upgrade their skills to get to the next level in their careers

I have worked with and seen them all. Wherever you are in life, it is okay.

During the career exploration process, I would teach students several tools to explore their career options, including:

1. Assess yourself. Take an inventory of your skills, values, and interests.

2. Find career fields that intersect with your skills, values, and interests.

3. Narrow down your career field choices based on what you find.

4. Explore these career fields. Find out whether the fields are growing or shrinking. Find out about the job opportunities and projections available in the areas you wish to live. Find out the projected salary information so you have realistic expectations about the amount of money you can make and the life you can afford to lead.

In the sections that follow, we'll look at each of these items in more depth.

Assess Yourself

Finding the right career for yourself is the intersection point between your skills, interests, and values. Your skills are the things you can do that you are good at. Are you good with numbers? Are you good at helping people? Are you good at problem solving? Are you good at working with your hands? Are you good at organizing, managing, or leading? Are you creative?

Your interests are the things you like to do. Do you like working with numbers? With people? Problem solving? Do you like working with your hands?

Your values refers to what is important to you in a career. Do you value knowing that your work makes a difference? Do you value a career that allows you to be creative? Do you value a career that allows you the opportunity to become wealthy or famous?

Many people struggle in a career because they lack skills or they are just not cut out for the job, even though they have an interest in it. For example, some people may want to pursue a career in the arts because they find it to be fun or exciting. Skill-wise, though, they may just not be very good at it. (Think of all those really bad singers at *American Idol* auditions.) Maybe they cannot sing or play an instrument or draw very well or their writing is poor, so a career in the arts is not something they are really cut out for.

Conversely, perhaps you are very skilled at something such as counseling. People always say you give great advice and feedback. Skill-wise, you have what it takes to be a great counselor, but interest-wise, perhaps you just don't like dealing with people.

Over the years, I have seen many people take on jobs and careers simply because they are something they are good at. Are these people necessarily fulfilled, though? Many times, the answer is "No" because while they may be good at it, it's not necessarily something they are interested in or enjoy.

The good news is that skills can be developed. That's why there are classes and training programs around. If you find a career field you have strong interest in but little skills for, it's not necessarily the end of your dreams. You can always train and study for it. If you wish to be a famous singer but don't necessarily have a great singing voice, you can always take voice lessons or get a degree in voice performance. If you want to fix cars, you can get a degree in automotive mechanics. If you wish to be a famous chef (or even a not-so-famous chef), you can get a degree in culinary arts.

Interests can also wax and wane over time. As youths, perhaps we wanted to pursue professional athletics, especially if we were raised as athletes. This pursuit may have piqued our interests in fields like exercise science. As we grow older and experience the ravages of time, perhaps our interests evolve to other fields like sports medicine or chiropractic.

I have seen many students enter college pursuing a certain field because it was the family profession. "All of my family members were service members/cops/firefighters/attorneys/mechanics/postal workers/truck drivers," they say, and that is all they've ever known. Those are all good and respectable careers, but we each have our own special gifts and potential, so I challenge you to discover what your gifts and passions are if you've not done so yet.

Various assessment quizzes are available for a modest price online or at your local job placement center or campus career counseling office. They can help you assess your career skills, interests, and values. I personally recommend the assessment services provided by Kuder through its website http://www.kuder.com. Another popular career inventory is the Holland Code. You can complete a free inventory through this U.S. Department of Labor sponsored site at http://www.mynextmove.org/explore/ip

Find and Narrow Your Career Fields

Upon completing your inventory of potential career fields, you should have a good idea of which careers you may be best suited for. Use the results as feedback for yourself. For some of you, the results may confirm what you already knew about yourself; you are, in fact, interested in or have an aptitude for certain fields. For others, the results may come out of left field and show you have an inclination for certain fields you never considered.

If you're undecided which career direction you wish to go in, use this opportunity to learn about yourself and the different opportunities out there. It's a wide world, and there's a place for each of us in it to build a fulfilling career for ourselves and our loved ones.

Explore These Career Fields

Once you've used your inventories and preliminary research to narrow down some career possibilities for yourself, take some time to explore the careers in depth. What are the salary ranges for these careers? What are the job projections in the years ahead? Is the field growing (green jobs), or is the field declining (print media)? What are the salary and job projections for your area? You may find that jobs in your field pay better or have more opportunities elsewhere. Are you okay with moving away from your family and friends to pursue your career, or does being close to loved ones mean enough to you that you'd settle for a backup career or job?

Set Your Course

A final thing to remember…you have your whole life ahead of you. That's especially true if you're a high school student. Today, people change careers or jobs an average of seven times in their lifetimes. This is especially true during our fast-changing and fast-paced world where new careers emerge all the time. Many of the jobs or majors available during my college years no longer exist because their industries have disappeared. Conversely, during my years working in higher education, I saw several new fields emerge and grow to prominence. You may find a field you love and are blessed to work in your entire life. Or you may find that the field your heart is set on may produce a nice career for many years, but because of how the world changes, it may become obsolete, forcing you to find another field down the road. You may very well be older and in the midst of a forced career change that's pushed you back to college again or to college for the first time. Wherever you are in life, you are right where you are supposed to be, and this is your time to set your course for the next phase of your life. Some of you are just starting out. Some of you may be starting over. Wherever you are going, I'm glad to be part of your journey.

> "A career path is rarely a path at all. A more interesting life is usually a more crooked, winding path of missteps, luck and vigorous work. It is almost always a balance between the things you try to make happen and the things that happen to you."
>
> — Tom Freston

YOUR COLLEGE AND LIFE ROADMAP

Finding a solid career direction is your first step in succeeding in college and life. Let's do some career exploration so you can find out more about yourself, what you are inclined toward, and how it can help you find the right direction in your studies.

1. Complete a career inventory such as Kuder at kuder.com.

2. Based on your inventory results, what are some of your job skills? _____
   _____
   _____
   _____
   _____
   _____

3. Based on your inventory results, what are some of your career interests? _____

_____

_____

_____

_____

_____

4. Based on your inventory results, what are some of your work values? _____

_____

_____

_____

_____

_____

5. Based on your inventory results, what are some possible careers that best fit you as inventoried on Kuder? _____

_____

_____

_____

_____

_____

_____

2
PICKING YOUR MAJOR

> "I was going to go to a four-year college and be an anthropologist or to an art school and be an illustrator when a friend convinced me to learn photography at the University of Southern California. Little did I know it was a school that taught you how to make movies! It had never occurred to me that I'd ever have any interest in filmmaking."
>
> — George Lucas

A Look Back, a Look Ahead

In the previous chapter, I discussed career exploration and how finding a strong career match for yourself intersects at the point where your skills, interests, and values meet. I shared career interest inventories you could take to evaluate your skills, interests, and values. From there, I talked about exploring specific career options, including salary ranges and job projections. In this chapter, I'll discuss how you can pick your academic major now that you have the added insight of which career path is the right fit for you.

What Does My Major Have to Do with Life?

Your major has everything to do with your life. The degree you earn in college gives you credentials in a field of study that will have direct bearing on your employment prospects and earning potential throughout your life. Many students often graduate, only to find that their degrees do not lead to employment prospects because they have earned degrees in fields where there is no demand for jobs. Studying something you're passionate about is important, but you also want to ensure that you are studying something you can parlay into a living, or if you choose to study something that does not lead to a career, you've thought that through and have other career plans in mind not related to your studies.

Finding the Right Major the First Time

For many students, one of the biggest barriers to finishing college in a timely manner is not knowing what they wish to major in, or they start down the path of one major, only to realize it's not for them, so they go back and change majors—sometimes even more than once.

While it's true you never know until you try whether or not something will work for you, ideally you want to identify the right major for yourself the first time out. You'll save lots of time and lots of money on wasted credits by finding and sticking to the right major the first time. The best way to do this is to do your career exploration upfront and identify the proper major to help you meet your career goal.

When I started college as an undergraduate, I knew I wanted to work within the media industry in either radio, TV, film, or web. Therefore, I determined the best major to give me that type of background was Communication. I also knew I wanted to start at

PICKING YOUR MAJOR 39

a community college because it was cheaper. I planned to do my "core requirements" at the two-year college, so I enrolled there as a liberal arts major. Then I transferred to a four-year college to finish my degree.

Because I knew what I wanted, I was able to "get in and get out" of college very quickly, finishing my bachelor's degree in just three years. However, it is not uncommon to see many students on the "five-year" or "six-year" graduation plan. Those students take longer for various reasons, including work and other commitments. Many, however, take longer because they change majors once or twice because they don't like or fail out of a major that wasn't right for them.

Ideally, you want to determine your academic goal at the outset. What credential do you wish to earn to advance in your career? If you've not had a chance to complete some of the career inventory work discussed in Chapter 1, you can go back and do that now. Once you are firm on your career direction, it will be easier for you to find the right major.

You Never Really Know Till You Try

Many students do not graduate on time for various reasons both beyond their control (such as prolonged illness) and within their control (such as failing classes because they don't bother attending them). One of the biggest hurdles for students in graduating on time that is under their control is switching majors midstream.

As discussed earlier, you want your major to match your career goals. Some pitfalls folks fall into that lead to mismatched majors and careers include:

1. Careers/majors that Mom and Dad picked out for them.

2. Family professions they have no personal interest in, but that everyone in the family goes into because it is expected.

3. Snob appeal professions that they "think" they want, but when they learn what those professions are really like, they are not what they really want to do.

4. Snob appeal professions that they just have no aptitude for.

Examples of snob appeal professions include:

1. Parents recommending to their kids to go into high-paying professions like law, medicine, or engineering because those fields make "good money." Making good money is always a nice motivator, but if you have no desire or passion for that field or your passions are elsewhere, your likelihood of wanting to put in the work required to be successful in studying and practicing in those fields is very low.

2. Some of us may come from limited backgrounds. Due to limited economic opportunities, perhaps everyone in your family worked for the same industry or company, be it auto mechanics, postal service work, the military, the hospitality industry, the airlines, a manufacturing plant, etc. As a result, perhaps you only saw a future for yourself in these industries. College is a time to explore, discover your passions, and take steps to move toward becoming your ideal self. If you're a person who always saw yourself capable of working in only one type of industry, I challenge you to explore your options.

3. Many people wish to enter certain professions because they are either high-paying (being a lawyer, doctor, engineer, nurse) or lead to chances at fame or fortune (being a

chef, fashion designer, musician, actor), but they do not necessarily have realistic information on the actual type of work involved in the profession or the likelihood of achieving said fame or success. No matter how you cut it, each profession involves hard work to achieve success, and at the end of the day, you need to be willing to put in the work required to succeed in that career. If you find yourself not really understanding the working conditions of your prospective profession, learn more about what you're getting into before you find yourself unpleasantly surprised and want to back away from what you signed up for.

4. Sadly, some people are just not cut out for certain fields. While skills are trainable, some folks, no matter how hard they try, just are not cut out for certain things. Engineering is an example. Lots of folks are attracted to engineering as a profession because of the respect the field gets and the chance for high compensation. With that said, engineering requires a strong aptitude for math and science, which for many folks is not a strong suit. If numbers and formulas, no matter how hard you study and work, are not your thing, engineering may just not be for you.

Direction Change

Ideally, after doing your career research and self-exploration as shown in Chapter 1, you should have settled on a career direction and identified a good major for yourself that you can stick with. This is the quickest path to finishing college on time.

Many students used to get off track by simply not knowing what they want to be when they grow up. They come to college undecided on a career or major and take a while to figure those things out. Sometimes, they come to college with a career and major in mind, but after taking a semester or two of classes and learning what the field is like, they find out it's not for them.

A friend from my undergrad years entered college intending to major in business and computer science because it was practical (business) and high paying (computer science). After struggling for a year with all the math needed to succeed in the major, and learning math was just not her thing, she did some self-exploration and decided that majoring in social services was more in line with what she wanted and liked to do because she loved helping people.

While I was majoring in communication, I had several classmates who switched majors into communication after not making it in similar but more rigorous fields such as engineering, computer science, or information systems. Some of those majors were too intensive in math or science requirements for some students so they found a better fit with a similar but less academically intense major.

Similarly, during my years working in higher education, I worked with lots of students who wound up changing majors midstream after trying a major they thought they'd be happy with only to find out it really wasn't for them.

Years ago, I had a student who initially wanted to major in automotive mechanics. After exploring some of the other majors we had and their earning opportunities, the student decided she wanted to major in diesel mechanics instead because she could make more money fixing diesel trucks than regular automobiles. She knew she was good with her hands and she liked fixing things. Being a female, she also stood a better chance to earn scholarships by majoring in this field.

More recently, I worked with a student who came to college positive that he wanted to go into nursing. Our college was renowned for its nursing program, and nurses are known to make great salaries. Upon exploration of our other majors and the work conditions in those fields, the student decided to major in radiology technology. The student knew he wanted to work in health care, but upon learning about more options, he decided being a radiology technician was more in line with what he could see himself doing as opposed to what he would need to do as a nurse.

Ultimately, it's okay to change directions if you try something out and find it's not right for you. That's life. We try, and sometimes, we find something is not right for us, no matter how much we thought it would be. There are always options out there. It's also okay to take up opportunities in similar or related fields we did not know were out there. Sometimes, we are limited only by our lack of awareness of other options. Take the time to explore what's out there for you. It's your life; be sure to seize and take control of it.

Take Your Time Finding Your Direction

Some of us will realistically need a semester or so to settle on a major. This is not a major problem in and of itself, and it is quite normal. If you need to take the first semester or all of your freshman year to decide on and narrow down a major, that's fine. Fortunately, most colleges have what are called core requirements—classes all students must take, regardless of major. Examples include English, math, history, etc. You can simply take your core classes during this time while you conduct your career exploration and narrow down prospective careers and corresponding majors without losing too much time. If you find yourself deep into your sophomore year, but you still haven't decided on your major, by that point you'll want to make a decision so you don't become lost in the "sea of indecision" and risk wasting tuition dollars or credits by taking courses you don't necessarily need.

To optimize your time and tuition dollars, though, it will work best for you to do all of this exploration during your high school years so you have a firm major decided upon when you first apply to college. Having a firm direction set early will save you time and money. I was able to earn my bachelor's degree in three years because I knew exactly what I wanted and had made the appropriate plans for which classes to take and when.

Create Your Own Major

One option you may consider if you are completely undecided and your college allows it is to create your own interdisciplinary major. One advantage to this is you get to study exactly what you want, provided the college offers enough classes to fill up your own custom-designed program of study. A more practical benefit of this approach is that the world is changing very quickly. Many fields that once had their own academic majors have disappeared as our society and world have changed. Conversely, many new fields have emerged that previously did not exist based on our changing societal needs. Recent examples would be the emergence of Green Technology or Sustainability Studies or Social Media, all fields that even ten years ago simply did not exist. If you're visionary and can predict trends, perhaps your own designed course of study could lay the groundwork for what will be a common major in ten years.

SUMMARY

The quickest path to graduating from college on time is to know what you want to major in upon enrollment. The longer you are indecisive on a major, the greater the chance you'll wind up taking extra courses you don't need to take or you'll find yourself caught switching between several majors, all of which lead to extra time in school and money spent on credits you didn't need.

Ideally, you want to conduct your own personal exploration into careers that are a fit for you. You can do this through the use of career assessments such as Kuder or Holland Codes or with the assistance of a guidance counselor, academic advisor, or career counselor on campus. Take the time to explore and learn about the options out there beyond what you initially saw for yourself. Lack of awareness of options can limit you.

Finally, despite our best efforts, sometimes we do need to change course if something we thought we would enjoy or could do simply does not pan out. If you need to take your time to explore, try your best to make a decision early in your sophomore year at latest because by that point, you are starting to run out of "core classes" and risk taking classes just for the sake of taking them, even if they are not necessary for your degree.

College offers you unlimited possibilities to reinvent yourself and become the person you were meant to be while also helping you to expand your mind. Whether you're looking to train for a new career or you simply want to expand your knowledge about a discipline, the key is to study what you're passionate about.

> "I can't change the direction of the wind, but I can adjust my sails to always reach my destination."
>
> — Jimmy Dean

> "The direction in which education starts a man will determine his future in life."
>
> — Plato

YOUR COLLEGE AND LIFE ROADMAP

Finding a major will impact your life and determine its direction. Let's take some time to think about prospective majors that meet your interest.

What do you plan to major in?

What are possible backup majors?

If you could customize your own major, what would it be?

Will your prospective or backup majors lead to careers in the job market? If not, what do you plan to do career or job wise?

3

SELECTING THE RIGHT SCHOOL

"For some students, especially in the sciences, the knowledge gained in college may be directly relevant to graduate study. For almost all students, a liberal arts education works in subtle ways to create a web of knowledge that will illumine problems and enlighten judgment on innumerable occasions in later life."

— Derek Bok

A Look Back, a Look Ahead

In the previous chapter, we talked about selecting your college major based on your career goals and aspirations. If it takes you a while to decide between certain majors, I recommend trying to make a decision by the end of your freshman year. In this chapter, I'll talk about finding the right college.

What Does Choosing a College Have to Do with Life?

Part of life success is finding out what is ultimately right for you. Whether it's the college you attend, the place you work at, the gym you work out at, or the eateries you choose to frequent, part of life is finding and choosing the environments conducive to your success; these environments must have the features and resources you need and be a right fit for your personality and style.

One often overlooked factor in college success is initially finding the right school. We are all different, so we thrive in different learning environments. First and foremost, find the school that is the right fit for you. This chapter will go over some considerations you will want to keep in mind.

Does the College Have the Program You Wish to Study?

First and foremost, does the college you are looking at have the major you wish to study? If you're not fully settled on a major just yet, do the schools you are looking at have programs or similar programs relevant to the career field you want to enter?

What Is the Program, Faculty, and School's Reputation?

Visit the college's website and review the program's website (if any) as well as the college's catalog. How robust does the program look? What types of courses are required and offered as electives? Read up on the program faculty. What are the backgrounds of the faculty? Check out RateMyProfessor to see what other students think about the faculty who teach in the program. Are the faculty respected and known in the field or discipline? Have they won teaching or research awards? How respected is the school you are looking at attending?

Check to see how well-respected both the institution and the program are compared to other schools. Is the college or program ranked nationally or regionally? Is your program accredited? Is the program respected in the community you wish to work in?

What Support Services Does the School Offer?

One major factor to take into consideration is the level of support services a college provides. The more services the campus has in place, the more places you can turn to for help when and if you need it. Some services you will want to be on the lookout for include: library/learning commons, advising/counseling, tutoring, peer mentoring, career and job placement, student employment, computer labs, printing and copy centers, disability support services, childcare services, and cafeteria and food services.

You'll also want to see whether the college provides additional support services geared for specific populations of which you may be a member. For example: Black Student Services, Latino Student Services, Native American Student Services, Asian or Pacific Islander Student Services, Alaska Native or Native Hawaiian Student Services, First Generation College Student Services, Single Parent Student Services, Multicultural Student Services, International Student Services, Immigrant Student Services, Women's Centers, LGBTIQ Centers, Veterans Centers, Former Inmate Student Services. Often, these programs provide aid to students within their target population, including but not limited to: tuition assistance, financial assistance with books or program supplies, computer labs or technology loan programs, tutoring or peer mentoring, and social support.

A crucial part of your success in college lies in your awareness of the support services your college and program provide to all students, as well as special services geared to students specifically like yourself, whatever your life circumstances may be. We will cover campus resources and support services in-depth in Chapter 6.

Having spent a good portion of my career working in student services, I have seen firsthand the effect support services have in leveling the playing field by giving students who normally might not have had a chance in college to succeed.

A student I once worked with was a participant in our Single Parents Student Support Service program. The Single Parents program helped her acquire financial aid specific for students such as herself to pay her tuition. The program also provided assistance in finding childcare, which allowed her peace of mind and time to attend classes. Finally, the program provided a referral for her to acquire an on-campus job, which was convenient and provided her with an income to meet and cover living expenses. Had the program not been available, the college experience would have been much more difficult, if not impossible, for her.

Another student I worked with was a participant in our Native Hawaiian Student Services program. We hired her to work as a peer mentor with other Native Hawaiian students. The income she earned allowed her to continue to support her family while studying full-time. She also developed her own personal leadership skills as a peer mentor. After earning her degree, she eventually became the director of a local preschool.

What Extra and Co-Curricular Activities Does the School Offer?

College is also a chance for you to explore and hone your interests outside of academics. Take some time to learn what types of clubs or

SELECTING THE RIGHT SCHOOOL 51

co-curricular programs your school offers. Are you in community service? Many schools offer service learning or service-based clubs. Are you interested in the performing arts, but you don't necessarily wish to major in the arts? If so, perhaps your school has a renowned glee club or drama club available. Are you competitive and athletic? Does your school participate in collegiate athletics? Perhaps you may luck out and get a scholarship to play for your school. Are you competitive and brainy? Perhaps your school competes in intercollegiate debate, mathematics, or science. I'll discuss extra and co-curricular activities in depth in Chapter 7.

Location, Location, Location

Whether you plan to stay home or go away for college, your school's location also plays a key factor in your success.

Is your school easily accessible for car or public transportation? If you plan to drive, how far away is it? Is there adequate parking, or will you need to park off-campus and walk? If there is parking, how convenient is it? If you plan to take public transportation, how easy is it to get there? How long will it take? Do you have a direct route, or will you need to transfer? Is your school directly on the transit line, or will you need to get off and walk?

If you plan to move away for school, where is your school located? Is it in an urban or rural area? Is campus housing available, or do you need to find a place to rent off-campus? If it's in a rural area, how far away are you from stores? How accessible or convenient is transportation to shopping and other key services not available on campus?

What type of environment do you think you can thrive in? Will a school in an urban setting be too busy for you? Does the peace and quiet of a rural country campus sound like a better place for you to study and excel? Conversely, does an urban school sound like it will give you the charge you need to forge ahead in your studies? Would a rural school be too slow for you?

Availability of Financing

We will discuss financial aid in depth in Chapter 5, but access to funding at your prospective school is important. Specifically, what you will want to learn is what types of scholarships or loans your institution or program gives to students like yourself. Federal and private aid will assist you to attend just about any institution. You will want to learn what specific forms of aid each institution has available and is willing to give you.

In addition to the above primary considerations, here are some others you will want to weigh.

Staying Close to Home vs. Going Away

Do you want to stay close to home, near family and friends, or are you aching to move away and experience life somewhere new? Few things help one to grow as a person more than getting out of one's comfort zone and experiencing life in a new environment. If you do choose to move away from home, though, prepare for homesickness and culture shock. For some people, being away from family and familiar surroundings can be heart-wrenching. For others, being somewhere new can be exhilarating. Moving somewhere new also gives you a chance to meet new people and experience different cultures. Others who are shyer may find not knowing anyone to be isolating. Ultimately, you need to know yourself and choose an environment where you can succeed. For example, if you are shy and have a hard time making new friends, you can either choose to stay home, go away with other friends, or work on your social skills until you can make friends easily. Homesickness is also less difficult today because technology is making our world smaller. Family and friends are only a text message, status update, Tweet, Instagram, Vine, Snapchat, Kik, FaceTime, or Skype away, which makes the distance much less than it used to be.

A Big Fish in a Small Pond vs. Just a Number

Another consideration is whether you wish to attend a small or a big school. Smaller schools have some of the familiarities of high school. Class sizes are smaller and you can get to know people better, including fellow students, as well as the teachers and staff. Larger universities, particularly in the freshman and sophomore years, are notorious for being places where you literally become just a number, especially with the required core or intro classes where you and a few hundred other students are attending class together in enormous lecture halls. Larger universities do tend to have more amenities and services on campus, but because of the size, many students often feel lost in the shuffle since it can be difficult to get assistance.

Public vs. Private

Another consideration is whether the school is publicly funded or a private institution. Generally speaking, public institutions will always be cheaper to attend than private schools. However, your financial aid package can defray large portions of the costs, whether you attend a public or private school. Most state schools are relatively interchangeable. Private schools run the gamut in terms of quality or prestige. Most of America's most prestigious schools are private schools. On the other hand, many private colleges are very tiny and run out of makeshift campuses in office buildings or strip malls. If you are planning to attend a private university, make sure the school provides the value for the premium you're going to pay in tuition over going to a public institution.

The Two-Year Start

A final consideration is possibly starting your college career at a two-year community college. Community colleges are a fraction of the cost of a four-year university, public or private, and they provide the small class size that many people find valuable for their success. Another added value is that community college professors' sole focus is on teaching as opposed to four-year institutions where teachers also must dedicate time to research. As a result, you may find that a community college instructor will have more time and energy to work with you individually.

My Returning to School as a Working Professional

Later in my life, once I'd completed my bachelor's degree and had been working for a year or so, I realized my degree was not enough to get the career entry and advancement opportunities I was looking for. At that point, I decided to receive additional training by pursuing my graduate degree. To achieve that, I decided on attending a local private university. Despite the extra costs in tuition, the private school's appeals to me were a wider availability of classes that fit my schedule and the accelerated timeframe in which I could complete my degree so I could get back into the job market quicker and with more credentials.

As the years went by, my career and professional goals constantly evolved, so I always sought additional learning opportunities. I would wind up going back to school a total of five times, earning credentials from three different universities inclusive of a graduate certificate and three master's degrees. At each point in my decision-making process, I always weighed out the financial cost to me, the availability of funding, the convenience of classes around my work schedule, and how quickly I could finish the program to continue advancing my career.

> "Like anyone who goes to college, you're leaving a familiar surrounding and a comfortable environment and your friends and everything, and you're starting fresh. It can be pretty daunting."
>
> — Jason Biggs

YOUR COLLEGE AND LIFE ROADMAP

Finding the right school will directly impact your success in college. Let's take some time and do some research to find the right school for you.

Does your preferred school offer the area of study you want to enter?

How respected is the program compared to its peers? How respected are the faculty?

Do you prefer to go to a smaller school or a bigger school?

Do you prefer to study in an urban or rural setting?

Would you consider starting at a two-year college as a means to save money and have smaller classes?

To assist in your decision-making process, use the table below to list your Top 5 school choices and the support services, extra and co-curricular activities, and financial aid packages available.

College/ University	Support Services Offered	Extra and Co-Curricular Activities Available	Financial Aid Offered

4

DEVELOPING YOUR ACADEMIC PLAN AND PICKING YOUR CLASSES

"Education is the key to the future: You've heard it a million times, and it's not wrong. Educated people have higher wages and lower unemployment rates, and better-educated countries grow faster and innovate more than other countries. But going to college is not enough. You also have to study the right subjects."

— Alex Tabarrok

A Look Back, a Look Ahead

In the previous chapter, we looked at considerations you should keep in mind when picking the right school for you, including whether it has your program of study, its location, the availability of support services on campus, and the amount of financing available to you. In this chapter, we will look at developing your academic plan, the specific courses you plan to take to complete your degree, and how best to select your classes.

Your Academic Plan

Quickly summed up, your academic plan consists of the specific courses you plan to take to fulfill your degree requirements. All degree programs have a prescribed set of classes you must take, as well as a prescribed set of elective requirements you must fulfill. For required courses, your choices are already made for you since you need those particular classes to graduate. Some degree programs only offer certain courses in certain semesters, which forces you to take classes in a certain sequence so mapping out your degree for those courses is preset. The area with leeway for you is your electives where you get to pick from a list of courses to meet certain requirements, usually in areas like languages, literature, sciences, and the humanities.

Picking Electives with Purpose

The purpose of electives is to broaden your worldview and knowledge base, so I encourage you to take classes from a wide variety of disciplines that personally pique your interest. If you can align these courses into your broader life and career goals, all the better. Foreign language requirements are a good example; it is a good strategy to take a foreign language that can lead to potential job leads or opportunities based on where you plan to live or work. Spanish is a good choice if working on the U.S. mainland. Other languages such as Mandarin or Japanese work well if you plan to work in Asian business. Arabic or Farsi is a good choice if you plan to work in the foreign service or military. Learning the languages of immigrant groups with a high immigration rate into your geographic area can also lead to good opportunities, especially if you are working in social services or translation services.

Arts are also a great area to develop skills in because you can often parlay your artistic skills into a second job or a money-making hobby in addition to your primary career. Whether you foster your creative writing, public speaking, acting, or dancing skills, or your drawing, painting, metal working, or sculpting abilities, I encourage you always to align your elective choices with your broader life and career goals or personal development interests.

Picking Classes for Success: Are You Ready?

Another consideration you want to keep in mind is to choose classes you are fully prepared for. One stumbling block for students is signing up for classes they are simply not ready for. Whether the class has too intense a level of writing, research, or difficult reading, if your writing, reading, or research capabilities are not up to par, you are setting yourself up to have a very difficult time or even fail. All classes list pre-requisite or co-requisite requirements that reflect the minimum level of preparation you need to enroll in the class. Many times, classes will also list a recommended requisite level. Pay close attention to these. If you're not at the recommended preparation level, it should make you pause and think twice about enrolling without getting more information from the instructor or department about the course.

Meet and Work with Your Advisor

Your advisor or counselor will help you to develop an academic plan and ensure you are on track in taking the right courses to graduate on time. It's recommended that you meet with your advisor at least once a semester. Once you get into your official major and department, often you will develop a good and close relationship with your advisor.

Research the Course

One strategy you can use to be prepared for the courses you want to take is to review their course syllabi. Departments often keep these on file, so you can request them. Many colleges now also make it a practice to post course syllabi online from previous terms. The course syllabi from an instructor usually outlines the readings, assignments, and exams required so you have a full idea of the workload and teaching style of the course's instructor.

Research the Instructor

Your instructor also affects your likelihood for success in a course. Find out whether the instructor teaching the course is a good fit for you. In Chapter 10, we will learn about learning styles. If possible, you want to find a teacher whose teaching style matches your learning style. You can learn about your instructor or potential course instructors through a few means:

1. Department websites often list short bios of faculty.

2. Request course syllabi through the department or directly from the instructor via email.

3. Attend a faculty meet or greet or schedule an appointment with an instructor. Often, departments will host meet and greet opportunities at the beginning of a term or during a registration period.

4. Talk with fellow students and get the scoop.

5. RateMyProfessor.com, through sheer bulk and aggregate, will often give a pretty good picture of what an instructor is like.

Building My Academic Plan

During my college years, I was excited to be in school. I bought the college catalog, read up on all the degree requirements, and mapped out my academic plan for my full degree prior to the first day of school. By planning out everything, it made my meetings with my advisor very quick and easy. While I didn't always get to take every class I wanted either because of class offerings and availability, having a plan with possible backups made it possible for me to get my degree ahead of schedule. By attending summer sessions and taking the class loads I had planned, I was able to finish my bachelor's degree in three years. The same was possible when I attended grad school for my MBA, M.Ed, and MPA degrees. Because I reviewed the course catalog and department websites, I was able to customize my learning experience by taking the courses I was interested in and learning the things I wanted.

The Dangers of Not Having a Plan

Based on my years of advising students, I can say that the students who lack a plan are the ones who usually do not finish or take a very long time to finish. Just like with traveling to get where you want to go, you need to know how to get there. In college, to get your degree, you need to know what classes you want to take and which ones you need to take. Motivated students who do this work in advance are the ones who succeed the most. Students who took the initiative to research and develop plans on their own made my job easy. Students who weren't too sure and needed assistance to develop a plan did okay once we had a plan in place. Students who never took the time to plan or always needed their hands held through the process often never finished or simply skated by.

SUMMARY

Your Academic Plan is your roadmap to your degree. It outlines the courses you need to take and when you plan to take them. You develop your academic plan in consultation with your academic advisor alongside information from the college catalog, schedule of classes, and your graduation advising sheet, which outlines all your degree requirements. In selecting electives, it's recommended you choose ones that help you further your life and career goals or open additional opportunities for you while also meeting your personal development interests.

Once you develop your academic plan, each term you can simply update your plan to reflect the courses offered. You can research courses and instructors through reviewing course syllabi, talking with other students, and using online information sources like department websites and RateMyProfessor.com

> "Planning is bringing the future into the present so that you can do something about it now."
>
> — Alan Lakein

YOUR COLLEGE AND LIFE ROADMAP

Setting a firm academic plan, researching your course requirements and elective options, and mapping out your classes each term will set you up for success. Let's take some time to plan out which classes you need to take and which you want to take.

- Are there any pre-requisite requirements you need to take to get into your prospective major?

If your major requires a foreign language requirement, what are you thinking of taking?

What types of science electives are you interested in taking?

What types of social science or humanities electives are you interested in taking?

What types of literature electives are you interested in taking?

To assist you in developing your academic plan, fill out the grid below with some of the classes you're thinking of taking each year and term. Consult your college's catalog of classes and the graduation advising sheets provided by your college's advising center.

My Four-Year Plan (or Two-Year if working on an Associate's Degree)

	FALL	SPRING	SUMMER
Freshman Year — Required Classes			
Freshman Year — Elective Classses			
Sophomore Year — Required Classes			
Sophomore Year — Elective Classses			
Junior Year — Required Classes			
Junior Year — Elective Classses			
Senior Year — Required Classes			
Senior Year — Elective Classses			

My Semester Plan

Take some time to research and learn about the instructors teaching the courses you have to take. Try to find a good teacher who's a good match for you. Repeat this exercise each and every semester until graduation.

Courses I Will Take This Term	Instructors Who Will Teach This	Ratings and Reviews of the Instructors	The Best Instructor for Me This Semester for This Course Is				
1. 2. 3.	1. 2. 3.	1. 2. 3.	1. 2. 3.				

5

FINANCING YOUR COLLEGE EDUCATION

"No one should be denied the opportunity to get an education and increase their earning potential based solely on their inability to pay for a college education."

— Bobby Scott

A Look Back, a Look Ahead

In the last chapter, we discussed planning out your classes each semester and the strategies you can use to pick your classes and instructors. In this chapter, we will take a look at how you can finance your education and the various people out there who are willing to give (or loan) you money for school.

What Does Financing a College Education Have to Do with Life?

In life, very few things are free. You will be called on to finance many things throughout your life, be it a car, a home, furniture, appliances, or your own children's education. Knowing where you can get money to finance the things you need is important.

OVERVIEW OF FINANCIAL AID

Financial Aid is the overall term that describes the various monies available to students to fund their college educations. Below, I'll describe the major types of aid available and give a broad overview of potential sources of funding you can look at when you start to put together your financial aid package. One thing you will want to realize upfront is that, given the cost of a college education, it will require work on your part to cobble together various forms of aid to pay for your college education, which means applying for any and all types of scholarships or loans that you qualify for.

The Financial Aid Cycle

One of the first things you will want to know is that financial aid is done in a cycle. You will need to apply for financial aid each and every year you are in the cycle, so you will need to get into the habit of beginning your search for aid annually, typically beginning at the end of each fall semester. Spring semester is primetime for financial aid since it is when most applications are made available and become due, with awards being made over the summer and processed in time for the fall semester.

While many scholarships are renewable, they are not renewed automatically. Most financial aid that is renewable is contingent on several factors, including:

1. You continuously re-enroll each semester and stay enrolled the whole semester.

2. You are actively working toward your stated degree.

3. You keep up your grades.

Many granting organizations, as part of your terms for accepting a scholarship, may require you to *repay* your scholarship if you drop out of school or take classes not related to your degree. Should your grades not be satisfactory, most granting organizations will pull your scholarship from you. Therefore, it's important to keep up your grades and take the right classes!

FORMS OF AID

In the realm of college financing, you basically either receive a scholarship or a grant. Your other major option is to take out a loan. I discuss the differences between grants and loans in the following sections.

Scholarships and Grants

Scholarships and grants are typically what most people have in mind when they hear the term financial aid. Scholarships and grants are free money gifted to students by an organization to help fund their college education. Because they are gifts, there are no repayment requirements. But because of their nature (free money), scholarships and grants are usually very competitive and require students to apply and submit various materials. Common materials needed for competitive scholarship applications include items such as personal statements, essays, and letters of recommendation from people, as well as submitting other forms of documentation to verify eligibility. You'll want to focus as much of your energy as possible on trying to earn grants and scholarships.

Loans

Loans are money borrowed from a lender that must be paid back at some point in the future. Depending on the terms of the loan, many don't need to be paid back until after you have graduated. Given the choice between grants and loans, you will want to concentrate more on funding grants before you take out a student loan. In terms of student loans versus personal loans or paying for tuition on a credit card, you will want to take out a student loan first before seeking a personal loan or a credit card payment because student loan interest rates are lower and tax deductible.

SOURCES OF AID

Various organizations offer financial aid to college students. In this section, we'll go over the various places where you can apply for grants or loans. From the government to community funds, non-profit entities, the military, the school you're attending, or the company you work for, there is no shortage of places through which you can finance your education. It's simply a matter of knowing where to look and submitting the best application you can.

Federal Aid

The federal government is the biggest provider of financial aid for college students. The government provides grants, loans, and aid in the form of work study, which allows you to earn college money through a job on campus. Access to federal aid begins by filling out the Free Application for Federal Student Aid (FAFSA). It costs nothing to fill out the FAFSA and can potentially lead to you receiving thousands of dollars in college funds in the forms of grants, loans, or work study. I highly encourage everyone looking at going to college to fill out a FAFSA each year.

Military Aid and Veterans Benefits

Both the United States Department of Defense and Department of Veterans Affairs are tremendous providers of financial assistance to current and former military service members, along with their dependents or survivors. Some options for those who would like to explore service to our country as a means to paying for a college education include:

- Military service academies
- ROTC (Reserve Officers Training Corps)
- Active duty G.I. Bill
- Reserve duty G.I. Bill
- National Guard or Air National Guard
- Veterans G.I. Bill

Let's look at each of these in more detail.

U.S. Service Academies

For high-achieving students looking at a career in the military as commissioned officers, the United States military academies (West Point, Naval Academy, Air Force Academy, Coast Guard Academy, or Merchant Marine Academy) are an excellent option to receive a free, Ivy League level education, strong in the sciences, alongside a military salary while studying. To receive an education, you will need to commit to five years of active duty service in the military. Among the admissions eligibility requirements, you will need a nomination from either your U.S. Congress member or the Vice President of the United States.

The Reserve Officers Training Corps

The Reserve Officers Training Corps provides military officer training in exchange for college scholarships. Students attend classes at regular colleges or universities with regular college students while also attending ROTC classes on campus or at a nearby campus, coupled with other military training classes. In exchange for the scholarship, ROTC graduates commit to a period of active or reserve duty status up to eight years in most cases, with x number of years on active duty and x number of years on reserve duty, depending on the individual contract you sign.

G.I. Bill

Active duty military members, reserve members, and military veterans are all eligible for college assistance through the Montgomery G.I. Bill. Benefits vary based on when one served in the military since the laws have changed over time, but active duty service members and veterans are eligible for assistance with tuition, fees, books, and living expenses for college, vocational training, apprenticeships, and other job training opportunities.

National Guard/Air National Guard

Students joining the state National or air National Guard are also eligible for various forms of tuition assistance both from the guard as well as the G.I. Bill. An added benefit of guard duty is that you are eligible to receive benefits even while in high school if joining the guard as a high school student.

Service Branch Specific Aid

In addition to military-wide education benefits, each service branch also offers specific education assistance opportunities to its branch members. You will want to inquire with each department for updated information on education assistance opportunities and eligibility.

State Aid

Many state governments also provide financial aid for students. You will want to explore any opportunities your state may provide.

Institutional Aid

Most colleges will provide institutional financial aid packages and opportunities to students. Aid will come directly from the institution itself in the form of tuition waivers or as grants or scholarships offered by departments or donors and administered through the college. Check with your campus financial aid or scholarship office for these opportunities and how you can apply for them.

Your High School

Your high school may provide scholarship opportunities for college. Check with your guidance counselor for any opportunities and how you can apply for them.

Private Aid

In most communities, a community foundation or community fund or other private foundation exists that administers scholarships and grants given by private donors for those who want to attend college. Talking with your school counselor, attending a local college fair, or doing a Google search should help you identify your local community foundations and how you can go about applying for funding from them.

Your/Your Parents' Workplace

Your workplace or your parents' workplace is another source of funding you should explore. Many employers offer tuition assistance programs for employees to seek higher education and training as a source of staff and professional development. Often, companies or industries with regular turnover also offer tuition assistance as a benefit to recruit and retain employees for several years while they work their way through school. Some companies also offer tuition assistance or scholarships to children of employees. You or your parents can inquire with your human resources office to see what, if any, tuition assistance programs are available to you or your family.

Discipline Specific Scholarships

Many scholarships are targeted toward students who wish to study a specific discipline such as the sciences, engineering, education, or social services. Most of these scholarship opportunities are either administered by the college itself, a community foundation, or the entity providing the scholarship. One universal source that often serves as a clearinghouse for scholarships nationwide is FastWeb.com. If you're looking to conduct a general scholarship search, FastWeb.com is a good start.

Athletic Scholarships

Being a winning athlete can be your ticket to a college education. Many schools with athletics programs provide scholarships as a recruiting tool for great athletes to play for their teams. These scholarships are very competitive, and while some students do get a full ride to play sports, full-ride scholarships are few and far between. If you are blessed to be a great athlete, you may very well be able to secure a scholarship, but it will need to be just one of the various forms of aid you try to put together to pay for your education.

Honor Society Scholarships

Being a nerd has its privileges! Most honor societies include scholarship opportunities as a perk of membership. These scholarships are highly competitive by nature (you are competing against fellow honors students), but being a member makes you eligible for these otherwise exclusive opportunities.

Whether you are applying for your high school honor society's scholarship opportunities or scholarship opportunities from the college honor society you are invited to join, cash in on whatever opportunities your brilliant academic performance has afforded you!

Employment as a Funding Source

Another overlooked form of funding for school is simply taking on, or keeping, your regular job. Most college students are employed at least part-time. While aid is available for tuition, fees, or books, people still need to pay for housing and food, so most folks still retain some type of employment while going to school.

Student Employment

Finding an on-campus job is a great way to earn money for school or living expenses. Most jobs on campus can be built around your class schedule, and being on campus can be convenient since you can access both work and class easily and conveniently with minimal commuting. You can check your campus Student Employment Office or Career Center or their websites for job postings. Job opportunities include work in campus offices doing clerical duties, working in campus computer or science labs, assisting in campus libraries, tutoring in tutoring centers, food service in dining halls or cafeterias, or other duties in residence halls and athletics departments.

Graduate Assistantships

If you're a graduate student returning to school, you can also explore applying for graduate assistantships. These positions typically offer tuition assistance and may offer benefits such as medical insurance, depending on workload. Job duties may include teaching, student advising, or other program support duties.

Federal Work Study

Federal Work Study (FWS) is a form of federal financial aid that pays you tuition assistance through work performed in an on-campus job. You apply for eligibility for FWS through your FAFSA application. If you are awarded Federal Work Study, you apply for a job on campus that participates in Federal Work Study, and your wages are paid through FWS.

The Benefits of Student Employment

During my undergrad years, I worked as a student tutor at my college's tutoring center. The job was convenient to my schedule and working in the tutoring center helped me with my own studies because I was forced to up my own academic game since my job required me to help others with their classes. The friendships I made at my tutoring job endured into my professional years and down to this very day. My tutoring job ultimately helped to launch my professional career in academia, which lasted for fifteen years.

Throughout my career, I employed dozens of student workers as tutors, lab monitors, mentors, and clerical assistants. All of these students were cream of the crop students who would go on to graduate and launch very successful careers in their respective fields as teachers, engineers, IT technicians, specialists, etc. All would view the convenience of a student job as a good means for financially supporting themselves while pursuing their studies and as a contributing factor to their college and life success.

Maintaining Your Career or Regular Job

If you're looking at returning to school from the job market for advancement opportunities, you may be weighing the feasibility of leaving your job or career to study full-time versus studying part-time while maintaining a full-time career or job. You may have a family to support or a mortgage to pay, so leaving a job or career to study full-time may not be feasible. Most college students work part-time, and many students study part-time while maintaining a career.

During my graduate school years, I maintained my full-time career with the university during the day while pursuing my graduate degrees at night. My employer covered my tuition and fees so I was only responsible for paying for textbooks. Because I had a family to support and a mortgage to pay, leaving my career to pursue my studies was not an option, but like many working professionals, I was able to balance the responsibilities of work, school, and family.

My full-time career still provided the financial means I needed to support myself and my family, and my employer was generous in its financial support of my studies. During my grad school years, I had many classmates who also juggled their full-time careers while studying, and many of their employers provided forms of tuition assistance.

Advice on Applying for Aid

When applying for financial aid, many providers will ask you to write a personal statement or other type of essay as part of the application process. Many will also ask that you solicit letters of recommendation from previous or current instructors, counselors, or other people who know you and can attest to your abilities, such as employers, coaches, or members of the clergy. Here are some brief tips for each of these parts of the application process.

Personal Statements

Here are some overall guiding principles for writing a personal statement that sets you apart from other applicants.

1. Tell your story and let the reader get to know you.
2. Describe your passions.
3. Include your values.
4. Explain why you wish to study in the field you are going into.
5. State your personal and professional goals.
6. Discuss some of the challenges you've overcome in life that will help you succeed.

When it comes to personal statements, what scholarship providers are ultimately looking to find out is whether you have a solid professional goal in mind. They are also looking to see whether you have a good sense for who and what you are and what you wish to contribute to your field or your community. Finally, they want to know whether or not you have the capacity and drive to finish your degree in spite of challenges. If you do not have a sense of who you are or a solid goal in mind in terms of your degree or career, then funders may not be willing to take a risk on you. Funders want to give money to help folks achieve their degrees and enter professions. Scholarship providers don't normally foot the bill for people who are still "figuring things out." Furthermore, if your grades do not reflect the ability to complete a class or if your background includes a lot of starts and stops or the inability to see things through to completion, many scholarship providers may consider you a risk to fund. Demonstrate that you can and will finish your degree. If your background shows a lot of starts and stops, convince the scholarship provider that you have learned and acquired the discipline and direction you need to overcome whatever challenges have held you back in the past.

Letters of Recommendation

In soliciting letters of recommendation, what financial aid providers are looking for are people who can ultimately attest to your ability to do academic work and succeed in college. They're looking for people who can vouch that you will go to class, do the work, and pass your classes. Ultimately, they want letters from people who know your character and abilities and can ensure the financial aid provider that you're worthy of their financial support.

When you solicit letters of recommendation, seek out instructors, counselors, or other professionals who can speak to the following about you:

1. Your ability to perform well, whether it's in academics, work, or on other types of projects
2. Your ability to meet deadlines
3. Your reliability—do you show up and follow through on the things you commit to?
4. Your ability to work with others
5. Your ability to communicate

In the past, I've had less than stellar students who did not leave good impressions on me ask me for letters of recommendation. In good conscience, I was not able to support them. Ultimately, if you are going to ask someone for a support letter, be sure your record of work with the person is worthy of support.

Know and Master the Financial Aid Cycle

Earlier, I explained that financial aid occurs in an annual cycle. Each part of the year, you should be doing something to prepare your financial aid package for the following school year. Here is a general timeline you will want to adhere to:

August/September: Follow up and ensure your aid has been processed and applied to your account.

October/November: Meet with your academic advisor to ensure you are making satisfactory academic progress toward your degree and are taking the right classes. Plan out your classes for next term with your advisor.

December: Research scholarships and loans available through the college and private providers. Start writing or updating your personal statements and essays.

January/February: Complete your taxes and fill out the FAFSA. Apply for scholarships and loans from the providers you found in your research. Continue to research other funding opportunities. Revise your personal statements and essays for each application as appropriate. Solicit letters of recommendation as needed.

March/April: Meet with your advisor and ensure you are making satisfactory academic progress. Research and apply for any additional scholarships and loans that become available. Revise your personal statements and essays as appropriate.

May/June/July/August: Follow-up on all applications. Accept all scholarships offered and follow-up to ensure they are appropriately processed and applied to your account.

SUMMARY

In this chapter, I discussed the various forms and sources of financial aid available to college students. All college students should fill out the FAFSA to access the wide variety of financial aid opportunities provided by the Federal government. Financial aid opportunities also exist from many state governments, college institutions, private providers, community funds, employers, and the military. No shortage of financial assistance opportunities exists to pay for college if you wish to attend.

Once you have successfully applied and received financial assistance, you will want to memorize and use the financial aid annual cycle to reapply for your aid package each year so you can continue to receive the funding assistance you need to stay in school.

> "While there are many obstacles that deter students from going to college, finances by no means should be the deciding factor."
>
> — Bobby Scott

Your College and Life Roadmap

There are no shortage of financial aid sources if you know where to look and apply. Let's spend some time putting together your financial aid package so you can afford to attend and stay in school!

Exercise 1: Federal Aid

Apply for the FAFSA at http://www.fafsa.gov

Exercise 2: Research Funding Opportunities

Research scholarship options from the following sources:

1. High School
2. Prospective College and Universities
   - School A
   - School B
   - School C
   - School D
   - School E
3. Community Foundations
4. Your Employer or Your Parents' Employer
5. Your State

6. Your Discipline/Major

7. Athletics

8. Your Honor Society

Exercise 3: Write Your Personal Statement

Start drafting a personal statement. Your personal statement should contain these elements: your major and career goals, how you've overcome difficult situations in your life, things you're passionate about, and ideas on how you can contribute to your field once employed.

Exercise 4: Get Letters of Recommendation

List three people whom you plan to ask for letters of recommendation for scholarships.

1. _____

2. _____

3. _____

Exercise 5: Serve Your Country

Would you consider the military or military service as an option for funding school? Which branch? Active duty? Reserve? National Guard? ROTC?

Exercise 6: Get a Job on Campus

Contact your school's student employment office to inquire about available positions if you are currently not working.

6

USING CAMPUS RESOURCES—BUILDING YOUR SUPPORT TEAM

"It is possible to take a population of students who are failing and whose schools are failing them, who are being written off as not being college material, and if they have the right support, they can all go to college and succeed."

— Mitch Kapor

A Look Back, a Look Ahead

In our last chapter, we took a look at the various ways you can fund your education. In this chapter, we'll explore how you can build the support network you need to help you stay in school by taking advantage of the various services and resources your school provides

What Does a Campus Support Team Have to Do with Life?

Part of college and life success is knowing and using whatever resources are available to you to your advantage. In life, we face many challenges that can hold us back. By knowing about and using government, charitable, and business services that we can take advantage of for free, nominal cost, or regular cost, we can enhance our chances for success. Part of your college success plan is learning about and using all the services available to you to help you succeed in your studies. Lots of dedicated professionals want to help you achieve your goals in college and life! Let's learn about services your school may offer that you can find out more about when you get there!

Instructor Office Hours

Perhaps the most valuable campus resource that many students neglect to take advantage of is seeing their professors during office hours. All instructors are required to keep office hours to make themselves available to assist their students who need assistance. During office hours, you can work with your professors one-on-one to ask any questions you have about class lecture material. If you are having problems understanding the material or required assignments, the best source of help is your instructors, so definitely take advantage of visiting and seeing them when they are free and available to meet with you personally. Office hours are usually published in your course syllabus as well as posted outside of professors' office doors. In Chapter 22, I will expand upon working with your professors, and in Chapters 33 and 34, I will discuss how your professors are invaluable in helping you to jumpstart and launch your career post-graduation. Seeing them regularly during office hours is the start of these future benefits.

Your Academic Counselor/Advisor

Based on your academic major (or lack thereof), you will be assigned to one academic advisor or counselor to guide you through your degree program. Your advisor will help you pick out classes or verify that the classes you are taking will be credited toward your degree program. In addition, your advisor may be able to advocate for you with your instructors, should issues with them arise, or point you toward relevant resources on campus or in the community if issues arise that hinder your academic progress. At a minimum, you should meet with your advisor once a semester, or more as needed. Depending on your situation, your counselor or advisor may become a very crucial and influential person in your academic journey. Regardless, though, your counselor is one of your biggest resources and a member of your support network who is there to help you succeed.

Financial Aid and Scholarship Office

All campuses will have a financial aid office that processes financial aid applications and awards. If you are receiving financial aid, you will interact with this office each semester to pick up your checks or ensure that aid has been received, processed, and applied to your account. Scholarship offices may be part of the financial office or separate from financial aid. If separate, the scholarship office will typically be responsible for posting scholarship opportunities offered by the institution or from outside government or non-profit agencies, and it will help you with application assistance and processing applications if institution-sponsored. Many times, the scholarship office may offer assistance to you with writing your essays and personal statements.

Your College Library, Librarians, and Library Resources

Most colleges will have a library or learning resource center. Various reference and resource librarians are available to help you find the right books, articles, or other resources for your class projects and assignments. Most schools will have reference materials as well as librarians dedicated to each discipline in which a degree is offered (e.g., sciences, humanities, languages, health, etc.). Get to know the reference or resource librarian who services your specific discipline area. This person will be very valuable when it comes time to do research and other class projects and assignments.

Your Learning Resource, Learning Assistance, or Student Success Center

Most colleges house some type of Learning Resource, Learning Assistance, or Student Success Center. Often, these centers may be a part of, combined with, or housed in the campus library. Usually, these centers will offer learning assistance workshops that provide help with things like note-taking, time management, study skills, reading skills, test-taking strategies, or research skills. These centers may also house the main campus tutoring program, tutoring center, or writing assistance center. In any event, they are invaluable resources you should definitely take advantage of to get ahead.

Tutors and Tutoring Programs

A tutor is a private teacher knowledgeable in a specific subject area or discipline who can provide private one-on-one or small group learning assistance to help explain or teach specific discipline-related concepts for students and learners who may not have understood concepts or content in class or who need further learning assistance. Most colleges and universities will either employ tutors or outsource to an online tutoring service to provide students with a level of needed learning support. If your school employs tutors, they can either be upper class or graduate level students majoring in or with a high aptitude in the discipline they provide support in, or they could be full-time professional staff at the college with degrees in their discipline areas. Many colleges today opt to outsource tutoring to a private online tutoring service due to costs. Many campuses also provide a combination of both on-site tutoring staff and online tutoring. If your college does not provide tutoring or does not have tutoring hours convenient for you, you can also hire a private tutor for yourself if the need arises. Many qualified private tutors advertise their services on campus bulletin boards or via other means such as Craigslist. Tutoring is offered in most subject areas, but it is most common in widely taken subjects such as English, writing, math, biology, chemistry, physics, history, and foreign languages. Tutors are usually found in libraries, learning assistance centers, tutoring centers, writing centers, or housed in specific academic departments such as English, math, science, or foreign languages. The most important thing to remember is that most colleges and school do offer tutoring services for most core academic subjects. If you find yourself in need of help, take advantage of the tutors available or find whatever alternative assistance you can.

Peer Mentors

Many colleges may have peer mentoring programs where you, as an incoming student, have a chance to interact with upper class students who are available to "show you the ropes" of how college and your campus works. Sometimes, the best way to learn is to learn from someone who has been there. Peer mentors can give you the inside scoops on the who, what, where, and why of your campus in terms of just about anything. If your campus has peer mentors available, definitely befriend some as soon as possible!

Professional Mentoring or Coaching Opportunities

Once you are enrolled and well underway in your specific major, many schools and colleges offer professional mentoring and coaching opportunities with working professionals in your field, many of whom are alumni of your program. These opportunities are provided to help you learn more about what it's really like to work in your field from a real world practitioner. These opportunities also allow you to begin building your professional network, which may lead to employment opportunities upon graduation. I'll discuss more about how you can develop your post-college career and job as a student in Chapters 33 and 34. Working with a professional mentor or coach is one of those steps. If your school provides this type of opportunity, take advantage of it!

Campus Jobs and Student Employment Offices

In Chapter 5, I touched briefly on the benefits of student employment. Campus jobs are conveniently scheduled around your class schedule. Working on campus has been shown to correlate to your success in completing your degree. Student employment also helps you meet your living expenses or puts spare change in your pocket. Typically, campus jobs are posted online as well as at the campus Student Employment Office or Career Center. If you are a graduate student, definitely consider a Graduate Assistantship if you are not otherwise employed. GA positions often come with benefits, tuition assistance, and/or a stipend, if not an outright salary.

Campus Career Centers

Most campuses have a Career Center, which helps you with things such as Career Exploration and/or Development. The staff can help you explore career fields if you are undecided on a career and/or major. Career Centers may also assist you with such things as developing your resume, cover letter writing, and job interview skills and preparation. Many may offer a Career Exploration or Development Course you can take as an elective. Some majors may require such a course to graduate or during the first semester as part of the introduction to the major. Career centers often organize career fairs each semester, bringing prospective employers to campus. Career centers may also post job listings from the community or assist with job placement after graduation. Many career centers may be joined with or co-located to the Student Employment Office.

Campus and Student Technology Resources

As a college student, you have access to a wide variety of technology resources to help you power your studies. Over my twenty-year career in academia, I have been in sheer awe of the number of technology resources developed since my days as an undergrad. I wish I'd had access to these things as a young eighteen to twenty-two-year old! I often tell my students that they literally have no clue how lucky they are.

First off, most campuses do provide computer labs or centers throughout campus for you to type and print out papers or to look things up online. If you don't have a computer at home, the computer lab will be invaluable to you. Most campuses will also provide Wi-Fi connections. If you have a laptop or tablet computer, you'll be able to get access online at school to do whatever work you need in terms of looking things up online.

You may also have opportunities to get software for free or at significantly discounted rates as a student. Your college bookstore or campus IT department will publish and post software you can either download or access for free as a student. It will also post the software titles and where you can purchase them from at student rates specific to your school.

Also be aware that you can purchase technology hardware at discounted student rates. Your college bookstore or IT department often has negotiated deals with specific manufacturers, vendors, distributors, or resellers for such things as desktop computers, laptops, tablet devices, or smartphones. Again, the bookstore or IT department will have published lists of what deals you can get and from where.

Finally, when shopping online or in person at a technology vendor, you can also inquire whether the vendor offers deals for college students for software or hardware. Take advantage of the cheap rates you can get as a student! We'll discuss technology in more detail in Chapter 21.

STUDENT SUPPORT PROGRAMS GEARED TOWARD YOUR POPULATION

Most colleges will have student service programs for specific student populations, such as First Generation college students, Native American Students, and International Students. Recognizing the unique needs of certain student groups, most colleges have invested resources to develop programs and hire staff to lower educational barriers or to support the specific learning needs of certain types of students. You can typically find out information about these programs on your school's website under Student Services or by doing a search on the college's website or via Google search. Information may also be provided in college marketing brochures or at student orientation. If you fit into any of these groups, definitely see whether your college has some type of program for your population and take advantage of any or all of them!

Minorities

Many colleges have set up programs specifically to assist and support students coming from minority groups. If you fall into any of the minority groups below, see whether your college has a program or center that works specifically with people of your background or identification:

- Blacks/African Americans
- Native Americans
- Alaska Natives
- Native Hawaiians
- Hispanics
- Asians and Pacific Islanders
- LGBTIQ
- Women

The scope of services provided by these numbers are phenomenal and may include:

- dedicated counselors
- financial aid specific for your population for tuition and fees, books, supplies, or living assistance
- sections of or seats in required courses set aside for you
- tutoring and peer mentoring
- technology access or technology loan programs
- social activities and outings
- social services referrals for childcare, healthcare, or housing assistance

As a minority undergraduate student, I was lucky enough to take advantage of these types of services. As a college faculty and staff member, I also spent many years of my career working in these types of programs, and as I've seen these programs develop over the years, I've been in awe of how they've grown in scope of service. I have seen the positive impact these programs have on students who might otherwise be disadvantaged in their schooling.

Students with Disabilities

If you have a documented physical, mental, or learning disability, your school, by law, will provide you with assistance. If you have physical disabilities, you may be accommodated with access to special elevators, desks, or seating arrangements, Braille materials, or ASL interpreters. If you have a learning disability, some of the accommodations you may be provided with include extra time for exams or dedicated tutoring. Colleges will typically have a disabilities office through which you can make arrangements. Documentation on your part will typically need to be provided through a physician.

Undecided Major Students

If you are uncertain about a major you're interested in, many colleges will also provide counselors dedicated to working with you. Most of them will help you identify your interests and provide information on majors that may fit you. In the interim, they will also provide you with guidance on what courses you should be taking to help you fulfill general education requirements or prerequisite requirements for a major you want to pursue. If you are having trouble deciding on a major, it is critical you get into a program for undecided majors or work with a counselor who can help you.

Freshmen or First Year Students

Many colleges now provide programs catered toward working with freshmen. Often, these programs hold New Student Orientation and are available throughout your first year to help you acculturate to college life and point you in the direction of where you need to go for such things as financial aid, counseling, or selecting your classes in conjunction with your counselors.

Transfer Students

If you are a transfer student, either transferring into your institution or planning on transferring out of your current institution into another, your college may have a transfer program available to assist you. For students transferring in, the transfer program may help with things such as campus orientation and course advising and selection based on your transcript evaluations. If you are planning on transferring out of your college to another institution, the transfer program may provide you assistance with such things as application assistance or course selection that may help you transfer into your prospective college better so you can minimize "lost courses" due to transcript evaluations and course articulation or equivalencies. One problem within academia when transferring between institutions is that many times your transfer college may not accept courses you've taken at your current school for its graduation requirements, thus forcing you to retake certain types of courses you've taken previously. Transfer counselors may know which courses are not accepted at certain colleges that students commonly transfer to, and they may be able to advise you appropriately, helping you to save time and money on courses that won't count.

Low Income, First Generation, Homeless Youth, or Foster Care

If you come from a low income background, are the first generation in your family to go to college, are a current or aging out Foster Care youth, or a homeless youth, many colleges may have a program available for you through the Federal TRIO program. These programs are in place to help people from disadvantaged backgrounds have better access or build the support systems they need to succeed in college.

The scope of services these programs provide includes:

- Tutoring and peer mentoring
- Study skills assistance
- Financial aid application assistance
- Academic advising and course selection assistance
- Transfer assistance
- Career counseling
- Finding housing for homeless students
- Cultural activities

Single Parents

Some college campuses may have programs dedicated to helping single parents. Often, the challenges of raising a child solo can pose a significant barrier to students. Services offered to single parents may include:

- childcare referral assistance
- financial aid geared specifically for single parents
- job placement assistance specific for single parents

- counseling
- tutoring
- social activities and support with other single parents

Formerly Incarcerated Students

Many colleges provide support services specific to the needs of students who were incarcerated and have been recently released back into the community. The scope of services may include:

- dedicated counseling with counselors trained in the needs of the formerly incarcerated
- assistance in transitioning to life in the community
- assistance in transitioning to college life
- peer mentoring with upper class students formerly incarcerated
- assistance finding housing
- financial aid application assistance
- scholarships specifically geared toward assisting the formerly incarcerated
- tutoring
- social service and healthcare service referral to campus or community resources

International Students

If you are an international student on a student visa, your campus will typically have an office to assist you. Common services include ensuring you are in compliance with your visa requirements. The staff may also assist with acculturation to life in the United

States through orientation classes and tours of the campus and surrounding area, as well as workshops on social norms and using the public transportation system. Many of the offices may also organize social activities to offer you opportunities to make connections with classmates. Many programs will often work in conjunction with the English as a Second Language program to help you acquire the language skills needed to be successful in your studies.

Second Language or Immigrant Students

Many colleges may also have programs set up to assist students who are immigrants to the country and speak English as a Second Language. Common services include extra assistance in learning English, tutoring, peer mentoring, technology access, counseling, and acculturation activities.

Student Athletes

Schools with athletics programs may also provide services to help student athletes maintain their grades to ensure they meet eligibility requirements to continue playing. By and large, the support services provided are tutoring for required courses. Many times, tutors will travel on the road with the teams for road games to ensure student athletes have the assistance they need due to students often missing classes. Counselors may also be available to student athletes who are versed in both campus policy for athletes as well as athletic conference league policies regulating student athletes. These counselors also may advocate on behalf of students with professors for accommodations due to travel or practice schedules. As an athlete, definitely take advantage of any extra or specialized support to make sure you can balance your learning needs, which should be first and foremost, with your passion for the game!

Veterans

Many colleges provide Veterans Assistance programs. Primarily, these programs offer counselors or support staff who are versed in providing information for you on your VA benefits and assistance in processing, meeting, and maintaining your VA benefit requirements. In addition, many campus VA programs may also provide such support as:

- education to all veterans on the range of VA benefits available to them or their families
- assistance in transitioning to college life
- peer mentoring with other upper class VA students
- social activities and support with other VA students
- referral to social service, healthcare, or veterans resources in the local community
- advocacy and education on campus on the unique needs of veterans with faculty and other students
- tutoring
- technology access

Armed Forces Service Members, Dependents, or Survivors

Mirroring VA programs, many colleges also provide support services to current service members and their families. Programs are geared toward helping service members and their families process and utilize the full benefits available to them or provide outreach support on base or during deployment. As detailed in Chapter 5, service members, their dependents, and their survivors have financial assistance opportunities available to them whether through the Department of Defense, their particular service branch, or the Department of Veterans Affairs.

Many colleges provide staff and services specific to the needs of service members and their families to ensure benefits are properly processed, used, and maintained. Outreach and support services are also often provided to make access to education more convenient to military members and their families on base or during times of deployment so they can continue to work toward their degrees.

Examples of services provided may include:

- assistance during times of deployment, including counseling, advocacy with professors, and distance education support
- referral to social service, healthcare, or military support organizations in the local community
- education and advocacy for the needs of military service members and their families on campus
- courses, counseling, tutoring, or technology access on base

ROTC-enrolled students are usually provided support through their programs to ensure they are in compliance with all requirements in regard to their scholarship assistance and service obligation requirements. Support is typically easier given the cohort nature of the program.

Food Services

Everyone has to eat! Just about all colleges will provide some type of food service. Regular schools will typically have at the very least a cafeteria. Bigger schools will have several dining facilities such as cafeterias or food courts with diverse dining options. Many schools may also contract with different vendors to bring food trucks or coffee carts on campus and provide more diversity and choices to dining options. Very small schools will typically provide vending machines or campus convenient stores that may sell small meals or be situated in areas with restaurants or convenience stores nearby. If you are attending a university with campus housing, a meal plan will often come with your housing. Sometimes, meal plans may be offered as an option to students living off-campus as well. As always, you may also choose to bring lunch from home or dine at any of the other eateries in the areas surrounding your school, or if you live near campus, return home to eat.

Transportation Assistance Programs

Many colleges provide some form of transportation assistance in conjunction with the local transportation authority or municipal government. Most public transportation systems offer a student rate for fares or monthly passes. Many colleges often negotiate deep discount rates for their students, making them eligible for special passes either on a monthly or by semester basis. Passes are usually sold at the student ID office or are part of the student ID if available on a by semester basis.

Many campuses also include shuttles that drive a route through the neighboring community from parking areas frequented or available to students. Local bus, train, or subway transit routes may also stop at college campuses, making public transit commuting convenient.

If you prefer commuting by car, many campuses also offer ride-sharing services or options to help connect students coming in from the same areas.

If you're not using public transportation, definitely consider a ride-sharing referral or arrangement because it'll help you lower your gasoline and parking costs. Parking costs alone on many college campuses or nearby lots can put a serious dent in your wallet.

Student Housing or Off-Campus Housing Assistance Programs

If you are attending a school with dormitory facilities, there will be a full housing office and residence hall or dormitory staff and advisors to provide all the support and assistance you need. Many housing programs will organize and provide services such as tutoring or social activities and support for student residents.

If your campus does not provide actual housing, it may provide housing assistance or an off-campus housing program to help you find housing in your neighboring community if you are a non-local student. Many landlords will work with campus housing assistance offices and list their available units or rooms to target college students in need of housing. One of the most harrowing issues for students moving away from home is to find housing, especially if student dorms are not available. Off-campus housing programs are an invaluable resource for connecting students to student-friendly landlords within the community who are willing and able to rent to students.

For campuses that offer Greek Life, you will find housing at the house of the fraternity or sorority you are pledged and admitted into.

Healthcare Services and Resources

Most colleges will have a staff nurse on campus. Colleges or universities with more resources may have a health clinic on campus. Many universities, particularly those with medical programs, may also have teaching hospitals attached to them. Campuses with staff nurses can provide rudimentary first aid care to students as needed for health conditions or minor injuries. Campuses with health clinics or hospitals have staff doctors who can provide exams and treatments for illnesses. Many colleges also provide mental health services for students as part of their health clinics or as part of student services and counseling centers.

As a student, you are also eligible for health insurance at student rates if you are not covered by your parents' insurance. Your local health insurance providers, health exchanges, or campus health centers can provide information on available plans and assist you with signing up for coverage.

Finally, many campus health programs provide free or low-cost contraception for students, along with resources and education on STDs and alcohol and drug abuse.

Fitness Centers

Many larger universities will have a student fitness center. Depending on the campus' size, the fitness center may give preference to student athletes for usage. Some larger schools may maintain facilities for student athletes separate from general use facilities for the rest of the campus. If you are fortunate enough to attend such a school, facilities may be free or offered at a nominal rate, often cheaper than or comparable to a commercial gym. You may see cost savings compared to maintaining outside gym memberships. In lieu of actual gyms, many campuses may offer exercises classes through Leisure Centers or as part of the academic curriculum as electives through a Kinesiology or Exercise Science department.

Childcare Assistance Programs or Referral Services

College campuses that offer an early childhood degree may also offer childcare on campus in preschool settings used as learning laboratories for early childhood degree students. Preschool tuition is often lower or competitive with commercial preschools. If childcare is not available, many campuses may offer referrals or have special rate arrangements made with neighboring commercial preschools.

SUMMARY

In this chapter, we explored the various campus resources available to you both from a learning assistance perspective as well as a student services support perspective. Colleges ultimately want you to succeed and earn your degrees from them, so they provide a multitude of resources to help you get through school. As students, take the time to learn about the various support services available to you and build the support network that will help you get through college. From your instructors, to your counselors, librarians, tutors, financial aid officers, peer mentors, career services and student employment officers, and from special programs to housing services and resources, childcare services and resources, transportation services, and healthcare services, colleges provide comprehensive support to take care of your learning and other needs.

"Be strong, be fearless, be beautiful. And believe that anything is possible when you have the right people there to support you."

— Misty Copeland

YOUR COLLEGE AND LIFE ROADMAP

Knowing about and utilizing your campus learning assistance and student service resources is a critical part of your college success game plan. This also applies to life and the many resources and services available in your community to meet whatever needs you have. Knowing and using your resources is a critical life success skill. Let's put together your resource plan for college!

USING CAMPUS RESOURCES

Exercise 1: Instructor Office Hours

What are the office hours for your instructors?

Where are your instructors' offices located?

Exercise 2: Your Counselor

Who is your academic counselor or advisor?

Where is your advisor's office located?

What is your advisor's contact information?

Exercise 3: Library Resources

Where is your campus library located?

What is the library's operating hours?

What are some of the services your library provides?

Exercise 4: Learning Assistance or Student Success Centers

Where is your campus Learning Assistance or Student Success Center located?

What are its operating hours?

What are some of the services it provides?

Exercise 5: Tutoring Services

Where are tutors available on campus?

What subjects are tutors available in?

Where can you find the tutors?

Exercise 6: Mentoring Programs

Does your campus provide a Peer Mentoring program?

If yes, where is it located?

Does your school provide a professional mentoring program?

If yes, how and where can you connect with a mentor?

Exercise 7: Student Services for Your Population

Does your college provide support services and programs for someone with your background?

How many of these programs are you eligible for?

Where can you find these programs?

What types of services do they offer?

Which of these programs and services do you plan to take advantage of?

Exercise 8: Food Services

What types of food services does your campus offer?

What types of dining options are in the surrounding community?

How much does the average meal cost at these various establishments?

What do you plan to do for meals on a regular basis? Will you take advantage of campus or community dining or do you plan to bring food from home or eat at home?

Exercise 9: Transportation

How do you plan to get to school every day?

How much will getting to school cost you daily? Each month? Each semester?

Exercise 10: Housing

Where do you plan to live? At home? On campus? Off-campus?

Does your campus offer student housing? How much does it cost?

Does your campus offer off-campus housing assistance? How much will you need to pay in rent?

Exercise 11: Healthcare

Do you have health insurance coverage?

If you need to get your own health insurance, what are your options?

Does your college offer health services?

Does your college offer mental health services?

Does your campus health services offer assistance with contraception, STDs, drug or alcohol abuse?

What are some of the services you plan to take advantage of?

If your campus offers limited health services, where in your college community do you plan to go for medical care? Dental care? Vision care? Prescriptions?

USING CAMPUS RESOURCES

Exercise 12: Fitness Center or Gym Facilities

Does your campus have a gym facility or fitness center? If so, how much is membership?

Does your campus offer exercises classes as part of the curriculum or through a leisure program? How much are classes?

Do you plan on taking advantage of workout facilities or classes?

Exercise 13: Childcare

Does your campus provide childcare if you need it? Does it provide referrals for childcare?

If you are in need of childcare, where do you plan to get it? How much will it cost you? How will you pay for it?

7

GETTING INVOLVED ON CAMPUS—MAKING THE MOST OF YOUR COLLEGE EXPERIENCE

"When I was in college, I wanted to be involved in things that would change the world."

— Elon Musk

A Look Back, a Look Ahead

In the previous chapter, I gave you a broad overview of the various support services available on campus to help you succeed in your studies and remain in school. In this chapter, I'll go over the various ways you can enhance your learning experience by getting involved in campus activities. While college's primary purpose is for us to learn the skills we need to enter our professions, the true college experience is not complete without friendships and experiences had outside the classroom.

You're Paying for Them

One thing to note about student activities on campus is that you're paying for them! Therefore, do your best to participate in whatever clubs, events, activities, or opportunities become available on campus. Not only are they good learning, networking, social, and developmental experiences that will enrich your life, but they provide practical skills that make you a better person and more attractive on your resume.

How are you paying for student activities, you may ask? In addition to your class tuition, you are also assessed a variety of fees. Some common fees may include:

- **Student Activity or Student Association Fee:** This fee goes to fund various events and activities for the school such as socials, concerts, tournaments, and other "fun" things, as well as your student government, which appropriates the fees.

- **Student Media and Publication Fees:** These fees typically go to fund such things as the school newspaper, campus radio or TV station, campus literary journals, student film or video organization, and anything else related to media and publications.

- **Student Union or Student Center Fee:** This fee typically goes to pay for maintenance of the campus center and the salaries of its staff.

- **Fitness Center Fee:** If your campus has a fitness facility, this fee typically goes to maintaining and staffing it.

- **Athletics Fees:** If your campus has an athletics program, this fee typically goes to things such as free or discounted admission to home games for students, maintaining training facilities, and paying athletics staff.

Student Organizations

Student organizations come in all shapes and sizes. Here I'll give a brief overview of some common organizations you can consider joining.

Student Government. Sometimes also referred to as student council, student senate, student congress, associated students association, etc., this is the governing body that represents student interests on campus to the college administration. Some of the things student government normally does or is responsible for include:

- representing and advocating for the needs of students to the school administration
- allocating and expending student activity fees, including requests for funds

Many students who have aspirations of a political career often whet their chops by joining student government because it gives them practical experience in representing a constituency, developing leadership skills, and learning about policy and governance. Even if you don't have any aspirations of a career in government, the experiences you'll have as a student leader are life-changing, and the skills you develop will carry you for a lifetime and influence your career. All organizations are always in the market for members and workers with leadership skills.

Throughout my college career, I spent many years in student government. The leadership skills I developed as a student leader carried me through many years of my career when I was able to assume formal and informal leadership positions, which led to career growth and advancement opportunities for me. The work as a student leader can be exhausting, frustrating, and often thankless, but the experience and skills you develop are more than worth it.

Student Media and Publications. These organizations run the gamut from publishing campus newspapers or news sites to running campus radio or television stations, printing student literary journals, operating and running student video or filmmaking clubs, and any other organizations that produce media content developed by and for students. Students interested in entering careers in the media as technicians, content developers, producers, directors, editors, or sales staff all find a home and practical experience joining a student media organization.

As an undergraduate, I majored in communications. Many of my classmates and those in our sister journalism program flooded the staff of the media and publications office and programs. Combined, my classmates ran the school newspaper, staffed the radio station, ran the video and film club and produced awesome films and documentaries, and published all the student literary journals. Whether it is writing; layout; graphics; copy editing; video editing; selling ads; producing radio shows or segments; recording commercials; developing ad copy; or filming movies, commercials, or music videos, if you aspire to a career in web, broadcast, film, TV, or print media, or you are just a hobbyist or enthusiast, you can't go wrong joining a student media organization.

Greek Life. When most people think of a student organization in colleges or universities, sororities for women and fraternities for men immediately come to mind. Joining a Greek society has many benefits. By and large, the most well-known aspects of Greek Life are the social ones. Membership in a sorority or fraternity basically guarantees a solid social life and support system while in school. However, Greek organizations also engage in leadership development, service work, and aiding you in your academics. Joining a Greek organization will provide you ample support and opportunities for growth as you assist in running a chapter and all the functions it undertakes. The connections you make will be lifelong because membership is lifelong. If housing is an issue for you, membership also gives you a place to stay since members typically are expected to live in the frat or sorority house. Beyond that, due to lifelong membership in a Greek organization, you will have a lifelong network to turn to over the years, thus opening up many opportunities for career advancement, business opportunities, or social support from your fellow brothers and sisters.

Honor Societies. Those who excel academically will be invited to join various honor societies, whether for general academics or various academic disciplines. Membership is always considered prestigious. Much like with Greek societies, honor societies are exclusive. Most honor societies emphasize scholarship, leadership, service, and fellowship. Participating actively in a chapter will help you to develop your leadership skills since all activities are developed and executed by members. An added benefit of an honor society membership is that you open yourself up to eligibility for exclusive scholarships since most honor societies maintain scholarship funds for members to continue their degree work. As with Greek societies, your membership is lifelong and opens you up to the professional networking opportunities available to members, including for jobs or business opportunities. Membership in an honor society always looks good on a resume, especially if you were inducted into a discipline-specific society in your career field. If you are tapped and invited to join a society, definitely accept the invitation!

During my undergraduate and graduate school years, I joined four different honor societies. As an undergrad, I had the opportunity to plan various service, fundraising, and fellowship activities for our chapter members. I also had the opportunity to develop my academic skills by undertaking the various scholarship activities the chapters undertook. These opportunities, along with the memories I made with my fellow members, stayed with me for years and contributed to my growth. I later applied these leadership skills to my career, allowing me to advance and later to start and lead my own company. Many of my fellow honor society classmates remain valuable colleagues and contacts to this very day. The relationships you forge do last a lifetime.

Band, Orchestra, Choir, or Glee. Very similar to high school, joining a college musical group is always a fun experience. Many of these organizations officially represent the school, particularly the band at high-level events such as football games. Many musical groups are independent clubs, but they may compete at the intercollegiate level, such as the glee clubs. Others may not compete but are active on campus, doing public performances for the campus or local community. Some may be private. Regardless of the level of public exposure, all are fun and bound to help you develop and build lifetime friendships with fellow music lovers. Some, such as the famous Straight No Chaser, an a capella glee club from Indiana University, may even lead to professional music careers!

Clubs (Academic, Religious, Social, Cultural). Most clubs may not be as high profile as student government, student media, Greek life, honor societies, or music groups. The vast majority revolve around some specific interest either in academics (major based clubs), religious, social, or cultural. Academic clubs are typically for students within a specific major so they can further explore and develop skills in their field (e.g., Psychology Club). Membership in such clubs allows you to network with classmates, expand your study, and get the help you need or offer help to other classmates. Religious clubs allow you to meet other students who share and practice your faith or are interested in deepening, expanding, or exploring their own faith (e.g., Bible Study Club). Social clubs are literally available for almost any interest, and they are good opportunities to meet people who share your social interest (e.g., Video Gamers Club, Chess Club, Car Club, Belly Dance Club, Zumba Club). Cultural clubs are opportunities to practice your culture or learn about another culture you've always been interested in (e.g., Japanese Club, African Club, French Club, etc.).

STUDENT ORGANIZATIONS BENEFITS
There are many benefits to joining student organizations. In this section, I will highlight some of those benefits.

Leadership Development Opportunities. You will have many chances to develop your leadership skills if you just look for them. If you join an honor society, developing leadership skills is almost a requirement and built into how the societies are run. The same will be true for student media or publication organizations, particularly if you accept a leadership position. Most student clubs will have a formal leadership structure with an elected board or some type of management structure made up of its members. If you accept leadership roles in your club, you will develop your leadership skills through the active management of club activities and formal governance.

Practical Skill Development. Depending on the organization, you may have a chance to develop practical skills that will make you more attractive in the marketplace. If your club organizes activities or takes on projects with deliverables, you will develop skills in event planning, organization, and project management. If your organization undertakes fundraising efforts, you will develop practical fundraising and development skills. All of these activities require leadership—a skill you will most definitely develop. If you are joining a student media organization, you will develop practical skills in the production of whatever digital, print, video, or audio media, or broadcast production you are charged with producing, thus honing your technical, production, and leadership skills.

Networking Opportunities. On a practical level, you are also ultimately building your personal and professional network. Like with your classmates in your major, many of your schoolmates in the student organizations you participate in will become lifelong contacts, colleagues, and friends. Often, the amount of work you undertake running and participating in a student organization is just as, if not more, grueling as your class work, but you'll build lasting relationships and memories with the folks who were by your side. If your club is more social in nature, the social bonds you form with others may last a lifetime as well.

Service Opportunities. Many of the student organizations you participate in may be service-focused. The work you undertake will make an impact on your community, and the folks you serve or organizations you partner with will expand your professional network. Organizing service activities requires strong leadership and collaboration. The work you undertake will increase your professional contacts and can lead to future work possibilities.

Social Life. As busy college students, particularly if you're going to school away from home, you may not have time for too much of a social life. Participating in a student organization will introduce you to many like-minded folks, and some of your club mates will become good friends. Your club membership and participation may become your primary social life outside of class.

Explore Interests. Participating in a student organization will allow you to explore and cultivate your interests. The beauty of a student club is that there is often a club for everything, and if there is not, you have the freedom to create your own club with others who share your interests. Perhaps you are already well-versed in an interest and simply want to connect with others who share it. Or perhaps you've always been interested in something, but you never had the time to explore it. Joining a club and meeting those experienced in it or other newbies is a great way to explore your interest while learning, growing, and meeting new people.

CAMPUS EVENTS AND ACTIVITIES

Colleges and universities, through the student government or student activities office, host various social events for students paid for from the student activity fees you are charged each semester. Larger schools, which collect more fees, are usually able to host a wide variety of activities for the student body. Some of the things colleges host that you will want to take advantage of (because you paid for them) include:

- **Socials:** These usually take the form of such things as picnics, barbecues, pizza days or nights, ice cream days or nights, etc. Basically, they take the form of fun social mixers and relaxers to bring people together and share some food.
- **Dances:** Like in high school, many student activities councils will host a dance for students to attend, often with a DJ and some food for attendees to enjoy.

- **Fairs:** These events will bring together a variety of clubs or vendors from on campus or the community to expose students to a variety of products and services they can take advantage of. Fairs will typically be focused on a specific theme (e.g., health fair, sustainability fair, craft fair, small business, etc.)

- **Concerts:** These will feature a well-known or upcoming local band or line-up of bands for your entertainment and to get your groove on.

- **Movie Nights:** Many schools will license and screen recent hit movies for your entertainment.

- **Game Tournaments:** Be it video games, board games, or intramural sports, you can count on some type of friendly competition with prizes and bragging rights on the line.

- **Karaoke Contests:** With prizes and bragging rights on the line, maybe you will be the next campus "Idol" or "Voice"?

- **Student Lounges and Game Rooms:** Just about all college campuses will have some type of lounge or games room where you can relax and rest or challenge your buddies to video games or vintage tabletop games like billiards, air hockey, ping pong, or foosball.

Leisure Centers

Many colleges may also run and staff a Leisure Center program that offers a variety of recreational classes for centers or personal interest courses. Some of the things you can look forward to if your school offers these include:

- Fitness classes like Zumba, Pilates, yoga, or martial arts

- Cultural classes like ethnic music, dance, or other forms of cultural expression
- Cooking classes

Depending on where you are in the country, your leisure center may also rent out recreational equipment for your use, such as skateboards, kites, snorkeling equipment, surfboards, or tennis rackets.

SCHOOL SPIRIT (ATHLETICS)

Athletics is big in colleges. Most universities and many small four-year schools will offer some type of division intercollegiate athletics program in most common sports for students to try for and compete in. Approximately half of the junior colleges in the country compete in junior level athletics. Even if your school does not compete in intercollegiate athletics, it may offer intramural sports. Let's talk about how you can get involved in athletics, whether you're a competitor or a spectator.

Be a Student Athlete. Being a student athlete opens many doors for you. You are immediately visible and in many ways a semi-celebrity, especially if you are competing in a sport with wide coverage in the media. Even if you are not in a big name sport, you are among the elite few who can juggle the demands of school with the demands of competition. The discipline you develop as a student athlete by juggling practice schedules and competition, coupled with the demands of the classroom, will forge your character and work ethic and carry you for years.

Health and Fitness. As an athlete, you will maintain your health and fitness, and develop the discipline and skills necessary for good health habits in your workouts and nutrition. In life, aside from your family, there is nothing more important than your health. Maintaining your health is critical to a successful life. Illness can have devastating impacts on your lifestyle and finances due to healthcare costs or missed earning opportunities. Take care of your health and develop good health during this time of your life. Playing sports can and will set you up with the tools you need.

Stepping Stone to Professional Sports. Very few of us will ever have the privilege of playing and making it in professional sports. One thing is for certain, though—just about all professional athletes were collegiate athletes first. If you have dreams of making the pros, you'll first need to don the uniform of your alma mater.

Scholarship Opportunities. Your excellence on the playing field or court may also net you the benefit of earning and retaining an athletic scholarship that will pay your way through school or be part of your overall financial aid package.

Attend Home Games. If you are not an athlete, definitely take the time to attend home games. If your school hosts games on campus, one of the best things you can do to take a break from studies and recharge is supporting your home team. It's also a great way to socialize with your classmates and friends.

Participate in Intramurals. If your school does not have field teams, consider playing intramurals. Intramural sports are games between teams comprised of fellow classmates against other teams within your school. You'll get a lot of the health and social benefits by playing, along with whatever bragging rights, if you have a successful team.

GET CULTURED

Most schools offer a variety of theatre, dance, or music classes. If you attend a larger school, these programs will often stage professional quality productions once or a few times per semester. You can take advantage of supporting your fellow classmates while enjoying great entertainment at a great price. Current students typically pay low prices for tickets compared to general admission tickets.

Student Theatre Productions. Whether it's Shakespeare, Broadway, Off-Broadway, independent, locally-written, cultural theatre, or student-written productions, student theatre productions are time well spent and provide great entertainment value for your dollar! Student productions are usually well regarded within the local community and are eagerly awaited.

Student Concerts and Recitals. Music classes typically stage showcase concerts at the end of each term for students to demonstrate their growth and skills. Students graduating, in particular, showcase their graduation compositions or projects. Admission may be free or at a nominal price. Again, if you're looking for variety in your music, these events are a great value for your dollar, and you get to support your fellow classmates.

Film Showcases. If your school has a film, cinema, or video production program, it will also typically offer a student showcase each term where classes screen their projects and productions. These events may be free of charge or have a nominal fee. If you love short films or documentaries or other wackiness caught on video, check out the works of fellow students and show them support while getting entertained or educated!

Student Art Exhibitions. Art departments usually hold showcases each term for students to highlight their portfolio projects. These exhibitions often serve food in addition to displaying the art itself. Admission is either free or at a nominal fee. If you love art, these exhibitions are must sees. Support your classmates and get cultured at the same time.

Literary Readings. English programs will typically have literary readings to showcase the writings of their students to the public. If you love stories, poetry, and other literature of the written and spoken word, attend these showcases to support your fellow students' creative endeavors and learn a thing or two.

SUMMARY

In this chapter, we talked about why you should get more involved on campus and how you can. Part of the college experience is experiencing all of the fun outside of the classroom, immersing yourself in college and campus life, and taking advantage of all the learning opportunities you have available to you in addition to your classes. All of these activities are funded through your student fees, so you are literally paying for all of this and should get your money's worth of fun and extracurricular education. Student organizations offer a variety of leadership, service, fellowship, and growth opportunities. Many of these organizations are career-building stepping stones if the work you do in them is related to your major. At the very least, they are all opportunities to expand and build your network. Campus events and activities like socials, concerts, and competitions are funded with your student activity fees. Collegiate athletics allow you an opportunity to compete in sports you love while maintaining and improving your fitness. If you are not athletic, they provide opportunities to build camaraderie with classmates while fostering school pride. College arts programs host productions each semester, providing you entertainment at a great dollar value while allowing you to support your fellow students.

> "College was the greatest four years of my life."
> — Jennie Finch

> "You never know when you're making a memory."
> — Rickie Lee Jones

YOUR COLLEGE AND LIFE ROADMAP

College is most memorably experienced outside the classroom. Research studies support and show that students who get involved in campus activities have higher graduation rates. Let's explore some of the activities you can consider getting involved with on campus and make a tentative plan for what you plan to participate in.

Exercise 1: Student Organizations

Look through your college student catalog or student activities website. What types of student organizations do you plan on participating in? Student government? Media or publications? Greek life? Honor societies? Social, religious, or cultural clubs?

Exercise 2: Campus Events and Activities

Look over your college student activities website or calendar of events. What types of activities do they sponsor throughout the semester? Which activities do you plan on participating in and attending?

Exercise 3: Leisure Centers

See whether your college has a Leisure Center or Leisure Programs. What types of classes or activities do they offer? What activities or classes would you be interested in participating in?

Exercise 4: Athletics

Does your college have an athletics or intramurals program? If it does, what types of sports or intramurals would you be interested in competing in?

If you're not the athletic type, where could you attend games? How much would they cost?

Exercise 5: Arts and Cultural Activities

Does you campus regularly produce student productions or exhibitions? Where can you attend these? How much do they cost? What types of productions are you specifically interested in?

PART II
COLLEGE SKILLS FOR SUCCESS

8

MAKING FRIENDS—THE POWER OF STUDY GROUPS

"I just want to thank everyone for their support. Sometimes friends need the help of their friends to get by."

— Richie Sambora

A Look Back, a Look Ahead

In the previous section, we took a look at college basics, including how to pick a major, the right school, your classes, and I gave you an overview of support services and student activities available in college. In this section, we will take a look at the critical study and college success skills you need to develop to succeed in college and, ultimately, in life since these skills will follow you into the workplace. In this chapter specifically, we will take a look at study groups and the importance of developing people skills and teamwork.

What Does Making Friends Have to Do with Life?

The ability to forge working relationships with peers and colleagues and to be part of a contributing team are important life skills you will be called upon to use in your career. Developing and honing your people skills are critical to your career and life success.

A solid social support system is also key to succeeding in college and in life. Your classmates will be a part of your social support system in school, and later in life, your work colleagues will be the same and help you thrive in the workplace.

On a practical level, forming study groups with your college classmates will help you to review course concepts and learn them better. One of the best ways to learn is to teach, and forming a study group allows you informally to teach and re-teach class concepts to each other. It also allows you to hold each other accountable for studying and to foster teamwork.

Finally, by participating in and thriving in a study group setting, you will develop valuable social capital and respect from your classmates, and you will potentially develop lifelong friendships and professional contacts that will help you with employment referrals in your future.

Your Current Classmates

When looking ahead to your career, keep in mind that many of your current classmates, especially those in your major, will eventually become your coworkers since many of you will be taking jobs for the same organizations throughout your career. Some of you may wind up working for the same company right away, while others may end up in the same workplace further down the road. If you do not work for the same company, you may work for partner organizations or competing organizations but run into each other at industry functions or trade association events. In either case, the point is you will be professional colleagues in the years ahead and continue to cross paths.

Some of your classmates may even one day become your bosses or supervisors. Many of them may be in the position to recruit you or offer you a more lucrative job than your current position. If your classmates have the potential to become your boss, you will want them to have positive memories of your work and work ethic while you were in school.

If you don't wind up in the same workplace as your classmates, they can still be part of your professional network. If you stay in touch, they may help you find a job or client leads from their own professional networks if you end up needing work, so again, you will want them to remember you for your solid work abilities.

Beyond being professional contacts, many of your classmates may become lifelong friends. Such relationships are something special to treasure.

Form a Regular Study Group

One of the best steps you can take to improve your success in any course is to form a study group with your classmates, or at the very least, a friend in the class whom you can contact for notes or assignment assistance. Ideally, you'll want to create a study group. To do so, identify the students who have a pretty good grasp of the class material and are responsible in getting assignments done on time. Do this within the first few class sessions and exchange phone numbers, emails, or Facebook contact information with them.

As the semester goes on and you near exams, use your study group to go over class notes and study guides and to prepare for exams.

Meet as a study group wherever it is convenient for you: the campus library or a coffee shop near campus or central to where your group lives, or if you can't connect in person, use a conferencing or chat technology like Skype, FaceTime, or Google Hangouts.

Some of the best memories I have of my college experience are meeting with classmates at the local pizza place over food and drinks or at the coffee shop or library. When I was in graduate school and other responsibilities made meeting in person impractical, the convenience of meeting online allowed our group to get a lot done while being time-efficient and still semi-social. Take advantage of the technology.

Be a Contributor

When working in a study group, it's key to do your best to be an active contributor. Come as prepared as you can, having reviewed the material, and have good questions about any areas you're not sure of. Be able to explain your understanding of the material so it benefits your classmates.

If you make commitments to your study mates to prepare materials or guides for the group, do your best to fulfill those commitments, or if unable, send a courtesy note apologizing for being unable to do so.

Finally, bring snacks if meeting in places without food. If you're not in a position to contribute to the discussion because you couldn't prepare or are completely lost, bringing snacks will be a nice way to contribute.

The main point is to be a contributor and not a free rider who shows up to get info but doesn't contribute to the group effort. People always remember and value the contributors and have more respect for them than those who just show up and "take" without giving.

SUMMARY

In this chapter, we discussed the critical role that forming study groups with your classmates plays in your college success, teamwork development, and group and relationship-building skills. Academically, study groups give you a support system so you can better learn and understand the material. Socially, groups help you build relationships, which is a valuable life skill. On a professional level, they help you build relationships with people who may be a part of your professional network throughout your career, allowing you to build social capital that can help your career. Your classmates may end up being your future coworkers or employers. Finally, we discussed the importance of being a contributor to any group effort and not a taker or free rider.

> "While we teach, we learn."
>
> — Seneca

YOUR COLLEGE AND CAREER ROADMAP

A study group provides academic support and relationship opportunities with your classmates that can drive your college and life success since many of your classmates will become your professional colleagues and lifelong friends. Let's start getting to know your classmates and making connections!

Find the smart, knowledgeable, friendly, and/or responsible people in your class whom you "click" with.

Exchange contact information.

Offer to form a study group that meets regularly in person or online.

9

MANAGING YOUR TIME— SO MUCH TO DO, SO LITTLE TIME

> "Lack of direction, not lack of time, is the problem.
> We all have twenty-four-hour days."
>
> — Zig Ziglar

A Look Back, a Look Ahead

In the last chapter, we looked at the value of forming study groups with your classmates. Study groups can help with your academic success by reinforcing and empowering your learning while also helping you to forge bonds with your classmates, many of whom, one day, will be in your professional network of colleagues.

In this chapter, we will tackle another key college and life success skill—time management. Managing your time is so imperative to your life success as you grow older and are forced to take on more responsibilities. Part of achieving life success and life balance is knowing how to manage your time well. I will introduce and explore time management concepts and strategies to help you succeed in college and in life.

What Does Time Management Have to Do with Life?

Time management is a core life skill. You are only given twenty-four hours each day to do everything you need to do: work, study, take care of yourself, take care of your family, travel, engage in hobbies, etc.

As you grow older, your responsibilities will increase as you progress in your career or start your family. You will need to learn to budget your time and juggle your various responsibilities within the time you have to accomplish what needs to be done. You can never escape from time management.

In this chapter, I will walk you through the steps you can take to get a grip on your time and master its usage.

Step 1: What Are Your Commitments?

The first step to managing your time is to take stock of all of your time commitments. From there, you'll be able to budget the amount of time you can dedicate to what needs to be done and see whether you are overcommitted (taking on too much); how you can economize your time; and whether you need to stop doing certain things to prioritize what needs to be done.

As a college student, you will need to juggle the demands of school with other life commitments such as jobs, family demands, social demands, and your own personal needs. Here is a list of common commitments that people, including students like yourself, may have on their time.

- School
- Job(s) or Career
- Family (Parents/Elders, Significant Other, Children)
- Social Life (Friends, Significant Other)
- Self-Care (Exercise, Hobbies)
- Sleep

As an undergraduate, I juggled going to school full-time and working a part-time job. As an educator, it was not uncommon for me to see many of the students I worked with juggle two or three part-time jobs while going to school full-time or part-time. During my graduate school years, I juggled working full-time, going to school part-time at night, providing for my family, and supporting the needs of my aging parents. Juggling all of those responsibilities was not an easy task, and it required a lot of time-management skills.

Step 2: Making More Time

"Deciding what not to do is as important as deciding what to do."

— Steve Jobs

We are only given twenty-four hours each day to do the things we need to do, and most of us have many, many, many demands on our time that we need to meet. Given all the things we need or want to do, the question often comes up, "How can I make more time?" You literally can't "make time," but you can free up your time with things you're currently doing so you can work on what you need or want to use your time to do. There are two primary methods for freeing up more time: delegation and deferment. In addition, you can also decline to do things that will take up your time.

As a student, your primary challenge will be making time in your schedule to study and complete your homework assignments. As such, you will need to figure out what you will stop doing to give yourself the necessary study time.

Delegate

Delegation refers to asking others to take on the tasks and chores you normally take on to free you up to do other things. As a student, some things you will likely need to delegate are any family commitments, including household chores such as laundry, dishes, grocery shopping, or providing child or elder care. You may need to ask spouses, significant others, siblings, or children to take on your share of the work to help free you up to complete your homework or studies. In the workplace, you may need to work with your supervisors to reassign certain more intensive projects to colleagues to help keep you from burning out. If you have a team that reports to you, you may consider delegating additional tasks to your team members.

Defer

Deferring of tasks is simply pushing back assignments that are not time critical. When analyzing your workload and tasks, you will need to prioritize the things you are doing and decide what will simply need to wait until you can get to it. If the task is not time critical, simply defer it to a later time in favor of getting done the things that absolutely need to be done now. You can also "defer" work by simply asking for an extension to get it done. If you have a paper or research project that you need extra time to complete because of work or family commitments, you can always ask the instructor for an extra day or two. He or she may not grant you the extension, but it does not hurt to ask.

The same principle applies in your workplace. If you cannot meet a deadline for a project and if there is wiggle room, you can always ask for an extension and defer the assignment a day or two. If laundry or yard work will take too much time and prevent you from completing your homework, perhaps you can defer doing your laundry or cleaning your yard a day or so if there's no one you can delegate it to.

Decline

The final principle to freeing up your time is to know when to say "No" to new tasks or requests that come up. You always have the option to decline a request. Ultimately, you must communicate your needs with regard to your time and responsibilities to the people in your life who expect things of you, be it your parents, your significant other, your boss, your instructor, or your classmates. Everyone is sympathetic to time and workload demands because we all juggle various commitments. If you ask for some support and flexibility, people will more than likely try their best to accommodate you.

Step 3: Schedule Time

The next thing you'll need to do once you've taken stock of all your commitments is to get them down on your calendar or schedule planner. You will want to keep a calendar of your activities and time commitments to help you build a routine, habits, and system so you can get done the tasks you need to.

Schedule Your Commitments

Get a calendar book/daily planner or use a calendar app on your computer or smartphone to schedule activities into your week and your day. Let's start by scheduling your weekly events that you are regularly responsible for:

- **Work time:** If you have a job, plug your work hours into your calendar.

- **Class time:** Plug your weekly class schedule into your calendar.

- **Commute time:** Plug in the times of your daily commute from when you leave home until you arrive at school or work. If you have young children, budget in time to get them to school.

- **Sleep time:** Schedule in your sleep time from when you normally go to bed until you wake up to start your day.

- **Schedule Specific Study and Homework Times**

With all of your regular commitments now laid out, schedule in your study and homework times in the evenings or on weekends. Make it a habit to dedicate specific hours of your day to only doing your homework. During your dedicated homework hours, limit time-wasting activities such as Facebook, Internet surfing not related to homework, playing mobile games on your phone, and social calls or chats. Ask your friends to limit their calls, texting, or IM during this time. Limiting your distractions will allow you to get more work done because you'll be able to focus more and not waste too much time on unnecessary things. You can always "play" later on Facebook or chit chat with your friends.

Now schedule any of your other life commitments into your schedule. Pick days and hours in your week that you can set aside to do some of the following:

- Family and household chores (cooking, cleaning, laundry,

grocery shopping, bill paying, and record keeping)

- Family activity time

- Social time with friends

- Self-care time (gym/workout time)

Step 4: Economizing Your Time

Another time management concept you can use is to economize your time. Economizing your time means making use of what is otherwise idle time to knock out additional tasks. Primary examples include commuting and waiting times or gym and workout times, especially during cardio times on machines or running laps.

Many folks commute via public transportation. I did so myself for many years. It would take me ninety minutes each day to commute from home to school and back. During that time, I would either catch up on my sleep and do homework during normal sleep hours, or if I could not rest, I would get some homework done while commuting. This is common for many students to do.

Workout times can also be a good way to economize. Many people use time on the treadmill, StairMaster, or other cardio machines to get textbook readings done or re-listen to lectures on their phones or mp3 players. If you're hurting for a social life because of school or work commitments, your workout time can also double as your social time with your friends if you work-out together. Part of keeping a balanced life with your school, work, and family commitments is building in enough "me" time to take care of your needs, such as working out or engaging in your hobbies. You can use some of your hobbies as social time with your friends if they like to engage in similar hobbies.

Step 5: Develop a Work and Task Flow System

Once you have your calendar set up, organize a work and task flow system. One of the best methodologies for this is David Allen's "Getting Things Done" system, popularized in his book of the same name. I highly recommend reading it in its entirety, but here is a summary of the workflow system he espouses:

1. Analyze tasks you need to do.
2. Analyze tasks and goals you want to do.
3. Develop a daily and weekly to-do list based on deadline.
4. Quick and easy items that can be done in a few minutes are "Tasks." Get these done first.
5. "Projects" consist of a variety of "tasks" or take longer. Work steadily on "Projects" over time.

You'll want to approach all of your to-dos, be it for school or your personal life, via this system. Schedule due dates and deadlines for homework, papers, and class projects on your calendar. For longer term projects, such as papers or projects, build some time into your scheduled homework time to complete them gradually.

For longer projects, set up milestones. Examples of milestones you can put on your calendar include:

- Conduct research by...
- Write first draft by...

Many times, your professors will include recommended due dates for such items as part of the course.

To help manage your life, you'll also want to build the following home and personal life tasks into your daily and weekly workflows:

- Grocery shopping
- Cooking
- Bill paying
- House cleaning
- Chores for parents, children, roommates
- Work tasks and projects
- Self-care (workouts, hobbies)

Step 6: Develop Daily To-Do/Task Lists

Once you've developed your task flow system of itemizing and prioritizing your tasks and projects, you'll want to develop a daily to-do list. You can use software for this on your computer or phone app, or put your lists together on paper—whatever works best for you.

To review, here's what you'll want to do daily based on our time management and GTD principles as taught by David Allen:

- Incorporate your task lists to form a daily task list for school projects and life tasks.
- Use a software system to help.
- Knock off the easy and short "tasks" first to get them out of the way.
- Work steadily to complete "projects" based on your milestones.
- Accomplish as much as possible.
- Delegate and defer items when possible.

With these systems fully in place, you now have a good, systemic way to manage your commitments, priorities, tasks, and projects.

Step 7: Delegate Out Tasks

Create time for you to focus on your studies by delegating out things. If you have chores to do at home ask your significant other, siblings, children, or roommates if they could take over the chores for the day. If it is within your means, hire out someone on apps and services such as TaskRabbit.

SUMMARY

In this chapter, I shared time-management concepts. I helped you to evaluate your commitments in life and organize your various school, work, family, social, and personal commitments and needs. I discussed how to calendar your time commitments and how you should schedule specific times during the day and week to study and complete assignments. From there, I went over the principles of delegation, deferment, and decline to free up your time to focus on your study needs. Finally, I covered some of David Allen's "Getting Things Done" principles to help you develop a systemic workflow system to complete your school and life tasks. These principles and tools will serve you well not only throughout your education, but your career and life as well.

> "He who every morning plans the transaction of the day and follows out that plan, carries a thread that will guide him through the maze of the most busy life. But where no plan is laid, where the disposal of time is surrendered merely to the chance of incidence, chaos will soon reign."
>
> — Victor Hugo

Your College and Life Roadmap

In this chapter, I laid out for you a time-management system you can use to juggle the demands of school along with the other commitments in your life. This system will enable your success both during your college years and beyond. Let's get you set-up!

Exercise 1: Create a Schedule

First, purchase either an organizer book/daily planner book or mobile or computer-based calendar system (Google Calendar, Outlook, iCal) that you can easily and regularly access.

Next, block off time on your calendar for the following commitments:

- Your classes
- Your job
- Commute time
- Sleep time

Now, block off specific hours daily to do your homework and reading assignments. Calendar in the deadlines for your project or paper deadlines. Calendar in the dates for your exams. Map out milestones to help you meet your project and paper requirements and test preparation.

Next, examine your home life to see whether you can delegate tasks or get assistance with other commitments (e.g., childcare, elder care, errands) from family members or trusted friends

Finally, taking care of yourself is important so schedule in some self-care time.

Schedule in time for exercise, hobbies, and social activities. Given other demands, you may need to cut back on these more than you are used to, but still make time for some form of self-care.

Exercise 2: Develop Your To-Do Workflow for One Week

- Examine your school, work, and family life to-do lists for the next week.

- Organize and map them out.

- Practice getting the short, quick, and easy tasks done first to get them out of the way.

- Knock away at the longer projects as you can.

10

KNOWING YOUR LEARNING STYLE—THE BEST WAY FOR YOU TO LEARN

"Know thyself."

— Greek proverb

A Look Back, a Look Ahead

In the previous chapter, we covered the critical life skill of time management, which will help you juggle not only the demands of college studies, but also the demands of life. In this chapter, I will discuss learning styles and help you determine how you learn best.

What Do Learning Styles Have to Do with Life?

Learning is a lifelong process. Long after you are done with school, you will continuously need to learn and relearn as life and the world changes. When you start a new job, you will need to undergo some type of training. As times change, you will need to relearn things or learn new skills. You may choose to take up new hobbies, which will also require you to learn new things. Knowing your learning style teaches you how you learn best so that as you are forced to adapt and change over time and learn new skills, you can get up to speed as quickly and painlessly as possible.

The Three Major Learning Styles

There are three major learning styles and, correspondingly, three different types of learners:

- **Visual:** You learn best visually (pictures, graphs, diagrams, videos, demonstrations)

- **Auditory:** You learn best through hearing (lectures, audiobooks, CDs, podcasts)

- **Kinesthetic:** You learn best by doing things physically (role playing, drawing, building, lab work, manipulating objects)

Ideal teaching and learning environments incorporate various visual, auditory, and kinesthetic learning modalities; however, just as you have your own learning style, your teachers will also have their own teaching styles, which may not include parts of all three styles.

People with different learning styles excel in different environments. Back in my undergraduate days, I signed up for a particular class with a friend who needed to take the same class so we got into the same section together. I enjoyed the instructor's engaging kinesthetic style since it resonated with my learning style. My friend had less stellar reviews for the class and lamented that he was more of a lecture type of person who just wanted to "hear" the information and found the activities too "fluffy." The point is, every one of us has our best way of learning and processing information. You want to identify what yours is and find teachers who can best match it.

Your Instructor's Teaching Style

Professors have their own teaching style just as you have your own learning style. Your instructor's teaching style may not match your learning style. Some examples of teaching methods instructors use that match with particular learning styles include:

- **Auditory:** Lecture talk with few visuals
- **Visual:** Lots of videos, slides, diagrams
- **Kinesthetic:** Lots of hands-on activities

Depending on the type of course or class size, kinesthetic learning activities may not be available or practical. This may be especially true for larger schools that have large lecture classes with a few hundred students in each section. Courses like that are almost exclusively lecture-based with some visual elements. If you're a kinesthetic type of learner, you may run into difficulties in such courses.

Learning Assistance

Knowing your learning style can help you compensate and reach out for the right assistance or resources to help "translate" the class material if you find a disconnect between the best way you learn and the way the material is presented by your instructor.

If several instructors teach the same course, you can find out which instructor's teaching style matches yours and register for his or her class beforehand. Reading reviews on sites like RateMyProfessor or simply asking fellow classmates can give you an idea of what types of instructional style your prospective professors use and how they match with the way you learn.

If you do find yourself in a class with a professor whose teaching style does not match your learning style, definitely take the time to visit with him or her during office hours. During your visits, let the professor know you learn best by your learning style and ask him or her to re-explain things that way or point you to the appropriate resources that can help you get a better understanding of the material.

Another strategy is to find a tutor or classmate who is good at explaining things in your learning style. You can go to your campus library, learning assistance, or tutoring center to see whether staff there have resources to help you learn material in a way that matches your learning style. Finally, you can always find resources online (e.g., YouTube videos, phone apps, etc.) that can help.

Take a Learning Styles Assessment

You can take many free and online learning styles assessments to determine what your learning style preference is. Your high school or college learning assistance center or program may offer learning style assessments and interpretations as part of their services to you. I highly recommended getting an assessment done as soon as you can.

SUMMARY

In this chapter, you learned about the three major learning styles: visual, auditory, and kinesthetic. A learning style assessment can help determine your preferred learning method. Instructors' teaching styles may differ from your learning style and cause challenges for you in a class. Knowing your learning style can help you "close the gap" if you are having trouble learning.

> "Tell me and I forget.
> Teach me and I remember.
> Involve me and I learn."
>
> — Benjamin Franklin

Your College and Life Roadmap

Knowing your learning style will help you better understand how you learn and can set you up for maximizing your learning by seeking out instructors or learning assistance that better "speaks" to the way you learn. Let's find out your learning style!

Exercise 1: Take a Learning Styles Assessment

Find out whether your school offers learning style assessments and formally take one. Have it interpreted by the instructor or counselor.

If your school does not offer that service, take a free one (or a few free ones) online.

Exercise 2: Note Your Instructor's Teaching Style

How does your instructor's teaching style mesh with your learning style?

How can you compensate in terms of finding other learning resources for your class if your teacher's style does not match yours?

Exercise 3: Find Campus Resources

- Visit your campus learning resource or learning assistance center to see what it has.

- Visit your campus library to see what resources it may have.

- Visit your campus tutoring center or program to see what resources it has.

Exercise 4: Check Online

- Look online for any videos or other learning aides that can help you.

- Look in your mobile app store (e.g., iTunes, Google Play) for apps that can help you learn the material better.

11

READING FOR EFFICIENCY—SO MUCH READING, SO LITTLE TIME

"Reading is to the mind what exercise is to the body."

— Joseph Addison

A Look Back, a Look Ahead

In the last chapter, we looked at the major learning styles, how they impact your learning, and how you can take advantage of this knowledge to seek out learning assistance or resources to help close any learning gaps in how course information is presented. In this chapter, we will take a look at reading efficiency strategies, another crucial college success skill since you'll be spending a large portion of time reading for your classes.

What Does Reading Efficiency Have to Do with Life?

Most information is transmitted in writing so you need to be able to read with efficiency. In many jobs, as in school, you will need to read and process lots of dense material in a short amount of time (e.g., manuals, reports, correspondence). Reading efficiently can help you process lots of information when you are short on time.

So Much Reading

College is funny in the sense that you pay lots of money to spend most of your time reading books and articles and writing papers. You will spend half of your time as a student reading. Often, there will be more reading than you have time to complete. If you find yourself in situations where you simply cannot get all the reading done, you may want to employ some reading strategies so you can partially read the chapters and articles you've been assigned. Obviously, it is better to get "some" of the reading done than none at all.

The Power of Skimming

If you find yourself in a time crunch and unable to read all the required chapters, you can skim a chapter and get some of the information you need. It's better to get an idea of what was covered in a chapter as opposed to blowing it off and not knowing any of the information.

How to Skim

Here is how you can skim a chapter. On the first run through a chapter, read the first sentence of each paragraph. This will give you a cursory idea of what the chapter or article covers. Do a second run through of the chapter and re-read the first sentence of each paragraph, but also read its concluding sentence. After this second run-through, you'll have a general idea of what the reading covers and its general themes to make a basic summary of what it was about.

Chapter Summaries

A final strategy you can employ is to read the chapter summary at the end of each chapter. Most chapters will have a summary at the end highlighting the key takeaways.

A Good Idea of What Was Covered

By skimming and reading the summary, you will have a general idea of what the chapter covered. While you won't have the full information and details, you will have a working knowledge of the main points. Skimming a chapter can be done relatively quickly. If you are assigned lots of very dense reading, skimming can be a good time-saving technique. If after skimming you find you have a greater interest in the chapter's material, you can always go back and invest the full time to read the complete chapter or article. If you find yourself with continued time crunches, taking the time to do the full reading may not be necessary. Most lectures recap the covered readings in detail so you will find that skimming and active listening during lectures will give you a thorough grounding in what you need to know for the class. In a perfect world, you'll have time to read the full chapter and learn everything you need to. In reality, this may not be possible, given other demands and responsibilities on your time, but it is better to learn highlights than not learn anything at all.

SUMMARY

In this chapter, we went over reading strategies for efficiency. It is not always possible to read all reading assignments given time constraints and your other commitments. Skimming can help you to learn a general overview of what a chapter covers. It is better to get some idea of what was covered than to skip a reading completely and miss out on information you should know.

> "Reading is a basic tool in the living of a good life."
>
> — Joseph Addison

Your College and Life Roadmap

Using solid reading techniques will help you process the vast amounts of material you are required to know as a college student. Let's practice the reading techniques we covered.

Practice skimming a chapter in an article or book chapter of your choice to see how well you understand what was covered.

Then go back and re-read the full chapter or article. See how well your understanding of the reading by skimming matches your understanding of the reading after you read the complete article. Were you on target with your understanding from skimming?

12

IMPROVING YOUR WRITING—PROPER WRITTEN COMMUNICATION

"Good writing is supposed to evoke sensation in the reader—not the fact that it is raining, but the feeling of being rained upon."

— E.L. Doctorow

A Look Back, a Look Ahead

In the previous chapter, we looked at skimming as a reading strategy to help you get through reading assignments when you're faced with a time crunch. In this chapter, we will look at how you can improve your writing.

What Does Writing Have to Do with Life?

From emails to letters and official correspondence, we do the vast majority of our business in society through the written word, whether it's for our jobs, business dealings with service providers, finding the right romantic match, or updating our social media accounts. You will write almost every single day of your life! Given this, you will want to master basic writing techniques while in school. Proper writing makes you look intelligent and professional. In this chapter, I will review basic techniques to help you improve your writing.

Writing—Lots of It

Along with reading, the vast majority of assignments in college are written assignments. Whether it's essays, reflection papers, reports, or research papers, you will spend a lot of your time writing something. As a result, you will get *lots* of practice writing and should be a competent writer by graduation. If writing isn't your strong suit now, don't sweat it too much; school is the time in your life to learn, work on, and master skills. You will have a chance to improve as a writer. In this chapter, I will give you tips and pointers to help you focus on improving your writing.

During my years in academia, I have worked with thousands of students and could see the progress they made as writers from the start of a semester to its end. In my own education, one of the most important courses I ever took was freshman composition. Coming into college, I thought I was a strong writer, but during that first semester of college, I learned a lot about proper writing syntax. My instructor, Sally Hall, helped me improve my writing tremendously. I still remember to this day, almost twenty years later, all of the things she pointed out and marked up on my papers, showing me what I was doing wrong and how I could improve my sentence structure and grammar. Ms. Hall was easily one of my most influential teachers, and here I am, twenty years later, publishing my first book!

The Best Way to Improve Your Writing…Is to Write

Like any skill in life, the best way to improve is to practice and actually do it. Practice makes perfect. Just as the best way to learn to play a musical instrument is actually to play it or the best way to learn to swim is to get in the water and practice kicking and stroking, so the best way to become a better writer is to write! If you're not confident about your writing abilities, just keep at it, and slowly, but surely, with practice and feedback, you will get better. Following are some pointers.

Write Every Chance You Get

Practice writing every chance you get! You don't necessarily need to write academic-related things. The main point is simply to write! You can write about anything and everything. Here are some ways you can consider writing to get started.

- **Journal:** Start keeping a journal and just write about your day and your feelings. People have journaled for thousands of years.

- **Facebook statuses:** In many ways, the Facebook status or Tweet is the modern way of journaling. When you status update, focus on using proper punctuation and grammar to help you improve your writing. Many people throw basic writing rules out the window when on social media.

- **Blog:** Blogs are the modern way of journaling in long form. It's free and easy to set-up a blog page, and you have full control over what you wish to write about, whether it's your hobbies, politics, thoughts on movies, music, TV, your cat or dog, or your kids.

- **Fan Fiction:** If you're bummed or disappointed in what

the official writers are doing to your favorite movie, TV, or book characters, you can always rewrite or expand upon the official stories in the realm of fan fiction.

- **Product or Service Reviews:** Share your thoughts on Blu-rays, new music, electronics, or the new restaurant or spa that opened in your neighborhood. Write reviews on Amazon or Yelp to help you practice and improve your writing skills.

There literally is no shortage of writing opportunities out there. Get out there and write, and focus on adhering to the rules of writing to make your practice perfect. I review the writing rules below.

Adhere to the Writing Formula

First things first, always adhere to the writing formula. As a quick review, every basic piece of writing should follow these rules:

- Have an "*Introduction*" that lets readers know what you are talking about (*thesis*) and why it's important.
- Discuss your first point ("*Point 1*") that supports your thesis.
- Discuss your second point ("*Point 2*") that supports your thesis.
- Discuss your third point ("*Point 3*") that supports your thesis.
- Discuss your fourth point ("*Point 4*") that supports your thesis.
- Provide a "*Summary/Conclusion*" of your main points with any appropriate call to action.

Adhering to the writing formula provides a solid and logical structure to your writing. It helps to keep it crisp, clear, concise, and on point, and it helps your readers to follow and understand what you're trying to convey. Learn and master this formula and you'll be a solid writer.

Spelling, Grammar, and Proofreading

In addition to mastering the writing formula, you will want to take time to learn the various grammar rules and work on your spelling. Spelling is fairly easy to improve nowadays by using the spell check features built into word processing software. Through repetition, your spelling will improve as autocorrect corrects any misspelled words for you. Grammar rules are also correctable through word processing software grammar checks, but they may take more time to master because you need to learn the specific rules. Your introductory freshman writing classes will help you with this, but depending on your writing level and whether English is your first language, this may take some work on your part. Use the spell check and grammar check feature of your word processing software every chance you get to help you out.

In addition, proofread your work to make sure it makes sense. Take the time to reread what you've written. Finally, have a friend or writing tutor read your work to see whether he or she can understand what you're trying to communicate. Writing tutors, in particular, are helpful because they usually are English majors or "A" level English students who have a solid grasp of grammar and other language rules. Since tutoring is usually a free service on campus, take advantage of it.

SUMMARY

In this chapter, we covered ways you can improve your writing. The more you write, the better you'll get. Write every opportunity you have, whether it's through social media (taking care to use full sentences with proper grammar), Yelp reviews, journaling, blogging, or writing fan fiction. Always adhere to the standard writing formula: introduction, main points, conclusion. Always proofread your work and check for spelling and grammar using your word processing software. Finally, have others read your writing to see whether it is clear and communicates your message.

> "Start writing, no matter what.
> The water does not flow until the faucet is turned on."
>
> — Louis L'Amour

Your College and Life Roadmap

Practicing your writing and adhering to best writing practices in terms of formulas, proofreading, and revision will power your success in college and in life as a written communicator. Let's set you up for success!

Exercise 1: Practice Writing

1. Practice writing in any format you wish: social media, journaling, a product or service review online through services like Amazon or Yelp, or a brief fan fiction piece involving your favorite characters. Get out there and write something!

2. Whatever it is you choose to write, be sure to adhere to the writing formula.

3. Be sure to run spell check and grammar check on your writing.

Exercise 2: Find the Writing Tutors!

Find and know where to find the writing tutors on your campus, the hours they are available, and the location.

Exercise 3: Get a Writing Buddy

Find a writing buddy who can help you proofread in addition to the writing tutors on campus.

13

TAKING GOOD NOTES— RECORDING WHAT YOU'RE HEARING

"I like to listen. I have learned a great deal from listening carefully. Most people never listen."

— Ernest Hemingway

A Look Back, a Look Ahead

In the last chapter, we took a look at ways you can improve your writing. In this chapter, we will take a look at note-taking. I will share with you some tools to help your note-taking and introduce you to some popular note-taking methods.

What Does Note-Taking Have to Do with Life?

At least half of what we learn or what is communicated to us comes through hearing. With our finite memories, we won't be able to remember everything we hear. We need a way to write down and record the things we hear so we can process them better at a later time.

In addition to school, many of the jobs we work require us to record things for further processing, whether it's minutes for a meeting we attend, a phone order from a customer, or a meal or drink order from a customer at a restaurant. In our daily lives, note-taking also comes into play, whether we need to keeps notes for an order we make with a company or customer service rep or a refund request. We need to keep timely and accurate notes. Note-taking is a critical life skill.

Let's take a look at some tools and techniques to help you become a better note taker.

Note-Taking Tools

Starting off with basics, you'll want to make sure you have the right tools to take notes with. I recommend and advocate digital notes because they are easier to keep and easy to back up so you don't lose them. I recommend using either a laptop or a tablet with a good note-taking software that backs up digitally. If you don't have the means to acquire a laptop or iPad, you can get by with a good old notepad, notebook, or paper in a binder with a pen or pencil.

Another tool at your disposal is to make recordings of your lectures. You can do this with your laptop, iPad, or a smartphone with the built-in recording software or digital voice recorder. Recording lectures gives you the luxury of re-listening to them if you need to while doing chores, sitting in traffic, running, or any other time of day.

Many instructors will give you PowerPoint slides or copies of their lecture notes, but it's still a good idea to take notes because the act of writing reinforces your learning. In addition, many instructors may also give you fill-in-the-blank sheets of the notes with the keywords to fill in. Instructors' copies of notes are a great tool. I highly suggest downloading or printing copies to review.

Recommended Software

If you are using a laptop or tablet device to take notes with, I highly recommend using "Evernote" software, which is available in desktop, web, and mobile formats. I have been an Evernote user since 2008, and I successfully used this program to help myself get through two graduate degrees. I like the way you can archive and organize your notes either in notebooks or with tags. The premium version allows you to record audio notes as well.

In lieu of using Evernote, you can also get by with other apps like Google Docs or a straight-up desktop Word document.

Lecture Formats

As you start to take notes, one thing you will want to keep in mind is that most lectures adhere to the standard "writing/speech formula" of:

- Introduction
- Main Point 1
  - Supporting Point 1
  - Supporting Point 2
- Main Point 2
  - Supporting Point 1
  - Supporting Point 2
- Conclusion

If you keep this in mind, you will be able to take better and more organized notes since you'll basically be filling in an outline. More on this later.

Note-Taking Concept

The key thing to do when taking notes is to write down the key points, ideas, and words your instructor shares. Knowing that the presentation adheres to the lecture format will help regardless of the note-taking format you use.

Note-Taking Methods

Four main methods of note-taking are popularly taught. They are:

1. Sentence Format
2. Outline Format
3. Map Format
4. Cornell Method

We'll cover each format briefly below.

Sentence Format Method

The sentence format method is basically a "line by line, play by play" of what the instructor says. You can think of it as if you're live tweeting your favorite show or sports game while watching TV.

Outline Format Method

The outline format basically follows the idea that lectures are typically organized and follow the standard speech and writing formula. You build a generic blank outline with key headings and subheadings and you "fill in" the outline with the main points and sub-points your instructor shares. If you use the outline method, you can set up your Evernote or piece of paper for each class with the standard Roman numeral style outline and just fill it in as you attend each lecture.

Conversely, you can also take notes in sentence format and then organize them into an outline. The outline format helps to organize notes into a logical and clearer format. And again, lectures, PowerPoint presentations, and instructor's notes are usually in outline formats already.

Mapping Format Method

The mapping method basically organizes notes into a mind map format with main points in a bubble and sub-points radiating from each key point in smaller bubbles. Mapping format works especially well for visual learners.

If you implement the mapping format for yourself, you can set up your notepaper into various bubbles and simply fill in each bubble as the lecture progresses. If using a software, a good mapping and visual software such as Inspiration, MS Visio, or Bubbl.us works well.

Cornell Method

The Cornell method, also known as the two-column method, is another popular format. The left column is a short column with the right column being a longer column. The short left column contains keywords and questions you note down during the lecture with the longer right column being for main ideas and other notes. The benefit of the Cornell method is that it allows you to keep accurate notes while also offering you an opportunity to reflect on what you're learning because questioning is built into the system. As you are listening to a lecture, you can also reflect and note down areas you're not too sure about in the left column as you go along.

SUMMARY

In this chapter, we took a look at the critical study and life skill of note-taking. We discussed the basic tools you'll need for note-taking, be it a computer or tablet with note-taking software, or paper and pen(cil). We discussed the four major note-taking methods: the sentence method, the outline method, the mapping method, and the Cornell method.

> "To read a book, to think it over, and to write out notes is a useful exercise; a book which will not repay some hard thought is not worth publishing."
>
> — Maria Mitchell

Your College and Life Roadmap

Get ready for college and life by getting your note-taking system in order.

If you have a computer or tablet, download Evernote or another note-taking software, or purchase a notebook, a notepad, or put some paper into a binder. Review each of the note-taking methods above or look them up online. Give each one a try until you find the method that works best for you.

14

PROCESSING INFORMATION WITH MIND AND CONCEPT MAPS—VISUALIZING CONCEPT RELATIONSHIPS

> "You can't connect the dots looking forward; you can only connect them looking backwards. So you have to trust that the dots will somehow connect in your future. You have to trust in something—your gut, destiny, life, karma, whatever. This approach has never let me down, and it has made all the difference in my life."
>
> — Steve Jobs

A Look Back, a Look Ahead

In the last chapter, we took a look at the various tools and methods you can use to take notes. In this chapter, we will get more visual; we'll take a look at mind mapping and concept mapping, two methods to help you visualize relationships between information to help enhance your learning.

What Does Mapping Have to Do with Life?

In life, we will always need to process information. When information is dense or difficult to understand, it helps to reformat it visually so we can see things better. Mind mapping and concept mapping are two tools that help you visualize the relationships between information and concepts. Utilizing these two tools can help you better understand concepts you are learning in your classes.

Mind Mapping for Brainstorming

Mind mapping is a tool to help you brainstorm by quickly getting ideas out of your head and down on paper. You basically jot down an idea into a bubble, and then jot down additional ideas that connect to the original one.

Some of the uses of mind mapping are:

- Working through writer's block while writing papers
- Visualizing outlines for papers
- Generating research topics
- Creative writing
- Generating ideas for anything

I was first introduced to brainstorming while in the gifted students program in fifth grade. Our teacher introduced it as a tool to help us come up with ideas for our science fair projects. I was reintroduced to it again years later in my college freshman composition class as a method to brainstorm our outlines for writing assignments. In my senior year in college, we used mind mapping to help us visualize and develop the navigation systems for websites in my web development classes. Years later, I was reintroduced to it in an introduction to comedic writing class I took for fun in a performing arts school. There we used it to brainstorm ideas for writing standup comedy and comedic sketches. Over the years, I always fell back on mind mapping to generate ideas and organize my thoughts, whether I was developing a new class to teach, putting together a class lecture, or writing a short story. Whether you're trying to write a paper, come up with topics to research, or develop a novel, brainstorming helps and mind mapping is a great method for doing it!

Concept Mapping for Learning

Similar to but a little more advanced than a mind map is a concept map. Concept mapping is a tool to visualize the relationships between various ideas by using connecting words between each bubble point to show and label the exact relationship between concepts.

Concept maps help you see the "big picture" and how ideas are related. They are a very effective study tool because they can really help you understand the relationships, causes, and effects between concepts, whether you're trying to learn science concepts, historical causes and effects, relationships between characters in literature, how systems develop and work, or any number of other things.

I was first introduced to concept mapping while an Information Systems student in graduate school where we used it to understand how database and software systems worked and to develop them on paper. I was later introduced to it by a good friend, also a programmer, who used it as a learning tool and exercise to teach his students the relationships between concepts in an organizational behavior class.

All in all, what makes concept mapping so powerful is that it helps you see the connections and relationships between concepts and to look at things from a systems level. As a student, you can use it as a study aid to help you construct and "put together" all the concepts you are learning in your class as you prepare for a final exam or to help you see from a bird's eye view everything you've learned throughout your program. If you are enrolled in a school that requires you to put together an ePortfolio upon graduation, showcasing and reflecting on all of your work, it may be a good tool to help you conceptualize everything.

Great Tools for Visual and Kinesthetic Learners

Mind and concept maps are also great learning aids for visual learners. If you recall from our discussion on learning styles, one of the main learning styles is visual learning. Mind mapping and concept mapping fit the learning needs of visual learners. Kinesthetic learners will also connect well with the process of creating mind and concept maps as a learning activity. The maps allow you to see concepts and their relationships, and the tactile creating of the maps will resonate for kinesthetic learners.

SUMMARY

Mind maps help students with brainstorming papers, researching topics, and any other assignments or projects where they need to generate ideas. Concept maps help you see the relationships between various ideas. Both are great learning tools for any discipline where you want a better understanding of the relationships between various concepts, such as scientific systems, historical causes and effects, relationships between literary characters, or IT or engineering systems. Both tools are great for visual and kinesthetic learners.

> "These are ideas. I could say that they just came to me, but it would be more accurate to say that I went to them. Ideas—and new connections between ideas—lead you away from commonly held perceptions of reality. Ideas lead you out here. Ideas lead you into the darkness."
>
> — Dave Sims

Your College and Life Roadmap

Mind mapping and concept mapping are two powerful tools you can use to your advantage as you work your way through college and in many other disciplines in your professional work or personal life. Let's practice making some mind maps and concept maps below.

Exercise 1: Mind Map Your Paper

Use a mind map to develop your next paper. Include:

- Thesis
- Point 1
- Sub-points
- Point 2
- Sub-points
- Point 3
- Sub-points

Exercise 2: Concept Map Your Course to Date

Develop a concept map of the concepts you've learned in your class to date. See whether you can draw the relationships between the various topics you've been learning.

15

MAKING STUDY AIDS— TOOLS TO SUCCEED

"You have to make your own condensed notes. You learn from MAKING them. A lot of thinking goes into deciding what to include and exclude. You develop your own system of abbreviations and memory methods for the information."

— Peter Rogers, *Straight A at Stanford and on to Harvard*

A Look Back, a Look Ahead

In the previous chapter, we explored creating mind maps and concepts maps to help you visualize what you're learning as a study aid and to help you brainstorm and generate ideas for assignments. In this chapter, we look at additional study aids to help you power through your studies.

What Do Study Aids Have to Do with Life?

Learning is a lifelong process. You will need to continue learning long after you graduate, whether it's something you need to learn for your job or you choose to take up new hobbies. Many professions may mandate continuing education requirements or require license or certification renewal of their employees. Learning never stops, so you will always want to develop the best learning aids to help empower your personal learning process. Knowing how to develop good learning aids will serve you throughout your life.

Let's take a look at some of the study aids, tools, and strategies you can use during your studies.

Types of Study Aids

One thing in our modern era that thoroughly amazes me is the number of learning aids available through the Internet and mobile technologies. My undergraduate career was during the late 1990s, during the Internet's infancy. While we had access to a tremendous amount of information during that time, over the last twenty years, the number of learning aids you have access to both on your computer and your mobile device has become astonishing. In this section, we'll discuss some traditional study tools that have worked for generations of students as well as some modern tools and modern spins on study aids now available. We will cover the following:

- Study guides
- Flashcards
- Online Information Banks
- Phone apps
- Language learning aids

Study Guides

One of the most basic study aids available is the generic study guide. Depending on the class you are taking and your instructor, a study guide may be part of the textbook bundle. Some instructors may also develop and distribute a study guide for each exam as a courtesy to you. In certain courses, instructors may develop study guides with you throughout the term. In other classes, you may be completely on your own in creating them.

At its most basic, a study guide is a compilation of your course notes. If you've utilized the note-taking tips outlined in Chapter 13, you can pull all your notes together to develop your own study guide. If you are working with your classmates in a study group, develop and update your notes among each other and use your notes to quiz each other prior to each test. Your notes are your best study guide.

Flashcards

Flashcards are an age old study tool. As an elementary school student back in the 1980s, I remember making flashcards with index cards to do both math and vocabulary drills for homework. If you're not familiar with flashcards, you basically write a question on one side of the card and the corresponding answer on the back. Flashcards are made for quick drilling of information and assist you with memorizing concepts. Flashcards lend themselves well to just about any subject area, whether you're memorizing vocabulary, definitions, or quick short answers to questions, and whether it's in a history, science, or any other type of class.

During my school years, we used index cards to make flashcards. Today, however, you can leverage technology to make them. If you have a smartphone, I recommend downloading a flashcard app to make flashcards for your classes where you need help memorizing information. Most of these software programs are fairly intuitive and easy to use. If you don't have a smartphone, there are flashcard website apps you can use to do the same thing if you wish to do them online. If that's not an option for you, good old index cards work just as well as they always have.

Online Information Banks

Many learning assistance or industry training companies provide online information banks full of information on their respective fields. If you are in need of specific information related to your course or discipline area, check with your tutors and instructors or with upper class students to see whether they know of information banks you can join and peruse for information related to your classes.

Websites and Phone Apps

One of the unique advantages available for today's student is the plethora of web and mobile device apps or learning resource sites you have access to. None of these were available to students when I was in college. Most academic disciplines have numerous resource websites or resource apps for your mobile device that you can access for whatever you are learning. Many are free or charge a nominal fee to download or access them. Your instructors or fellow classmates may be able to recommend good sites or apps to you. If you are not certain, look up and read reviews before you buy.

Nowadays, many colleges, learning centers, and libraries invest in many of these resource sites and services to assist students. At the university where I worked, we regularly bought into various learning aid libraries and services to provide needed learning assistance resources for students. Many of these resources also have subscriptions available to individuals. The main point is there is no lack of learning aids available to you in this day and age, regardless of what you are studying. Many of them are accessible at the touch of your finger online or on your phone. That puts you at a much greater advantage than what the people my age or older had when we were college students.

Language Learning Aids

Most of you will be required to take a foreign language as part of your graduation requirements, so I want to share some language learning tips with you. When learning a language, you need to learn a few skills:

- vocabulary building
- sentence structure and grammar
- listening
- reading
- speaking
- writing

For vocabulary building, flashcards help tremendously. Another tip is to immerse yourself in using the language. One simple way to do so is to label common everyday objects in your home or office with a notecard with the foreign language word for it. By doing this, you begin to immerse yourself and can immediately remember and apply the new vocabulary word and relate it to something you know.

Another way to immerse yourself is to change the language interface for your Facebook to the language you are studying. If you are daring, you might also change the interface for your phone or computer. Changing language interfaces will help your practical reading skills and vocabulary building. The more you immerse yourself in the language, the better you will learn it.

To develop your listening skills, I recommend finding music, movies, or television shows online in the language you are studying. You will develop your listening skills and, in turn, develop your speaking skills because you will know what the language sounds like.

Many language exchange websites also exist where you can meet native speakers in the language you are studying. Take some time to visit them and meet new folks whose language you can practice.

A final resource that is ever growing is Google translate. It can offer you assistance in translating from English to a second language.

SUMMARY

In this chapter, we discussed study aids. We talked about compiling your notes into a study guide for your exams if your instructor does not provide a study guide. We also discussed using flashcards to drill course concepts; you can use index cards, a mobile app, or other online apps to develop flashcards. We talked about online and mobile resources available for various subjects and disciplines. Finally, we talked about various strategies you can use when learning a foreign language for vocabulary building, language exchange, and language immersion.

> "You don't learn to walk by following rules.
> You learn by doing, and by falling over."
>
> — Richard Branson

Your College and Life Roadmap

Let's work on setting up some study aids to practice what we just learned!

Exercise 1: Study Guides

Take some time to put together your class notes for a class you're currently taking. Try to anticipate some questions your instructor will ask based on your notes. Keep a running tab of these questions and there you have your basic study guide.

Exercise 2: Flashcards

If you have a smartphone or a tablet device, download a flashcard app from the iTunes Store or Google Play. If you don't have access to a smartphone or tablet, purchase a deck of index cards. Start putting together a practice set of flashcards for a class you are currently taking.

Exercise 3: Online and Mobile Resources

Pick a class you are currently having some challenges in. Search the web or your mobile device store to see whether any resource sites or apps provide information you can use.

Exercise 4: Language Learning

Start labeling things around your home or office with the vocabulary words for them in the language you are studying. Develop some flashcards for common vocabulary words you are learning. Find some music, TV shows, or movies in the language you are learning. Finally, see whether you can find a language exchange resource site or community online to practice your language skills with a native speaker.

16

PREPARING FOR TESTS AND EXAMS—ARE YOU READY?

> "Forewarned, forearmed; to be prepared is half the victory."
>
> — Miguel de Cervantes

A Look Back, a Look Ahead

In the last chapter, I gave you an overview of the various study aids you can put together or access to empower your learning. From study guides to flashcards, online resources, mobile apps, and various language learning tips, you learned about tools that have worked for generations of students and more recent innovations. In this chapter, we will take these learning tips a step further and apply them to where it counts—test and exam preparation.

What Does Test and Exam Preparation Have to Do with Life?

Very few people have a lot of love for tests and exams, but they are a fact of life. Even after you finish school, chances are you will still be required to take tests or exams on occasion. Often, you will be required to test for advancement purposes or even to maintain your profession. Within your chosen profession, you may be required to sit for licensing or certification exams or renewal exams in order to remain employable or allowed to practice in your field. Your employers may require you to take occasional tests or exams. If you take up a hobby such as martial arts, you may be required to take exams for promotions. Even for things many of us take for granted, such as a driver's license, you are required to take a test. Tests and exams are a part of life.

Below are some tips for test and exam preparation.

Don't Stress Yourself Out

First and foremost, don't stress yourself out getting ready for tests. Over the years, I have seen thousands of students fret and fluster themselves when preparing for tests. Getting all bent out of shape only causes needless anxiety. Prepare as best as you can and take tests seriously, but don't let the pressure go to your head and cause you anxiety. Save yourself some needless stress and worry by keeping things in perspective. Tests are supposed to measure your learning. Many subject matters take time to master, so as someone who is still learning, cut yourself some slack if you don't get an A. B grades are fine. Even a C grade is okay. The main thing is that you've learned something during your time in a course. If you leave a course knowing more about the subject matter than you knew when you started, you've made progress.

With that said, let's take a look at some strategies you can use to prepare and nail for yourself the best grade possible.

Anticipate the Questions

One of the first things you should do is anticipate the questions your exams will ask. I alluded to this in the last chapter on learning aids and study guides. Take time to review your notes from each lecture. If your instructor gives you weekly quizzes, review the quiz questions and answers. More than likely, you will see quiz questions repeated on tests and exams. By and large, most of the questions your instructors ask will be from material covered within each lecture. Go back and review everything, and then write out questions covering the key terms, ideas, and concepts you've learned in each lecture. If you can answer practice questions for each key term, concept, or point, you'll be in good shape. Use your flashcards as a preparation tool.

Many of the questions you've anticipated will be on the exams. You'll do fine and may surprise yourself by how accurately you predict the questions you will see.

Anticipate the Question Types

Anticipating the question types is another thing you can do. Most tests basically follow the same formats in terms of question types: matching, fill in the blank, short answer, and essay.

For matching and fill in the blank questions, typically you'll want to study your definitions, key words, and key concepts for your subject matter.

Short answer and essay questions will require you to know the content in more depth and be able to explain things such as cause and effect and apply your own analysis to issues. With regard to short answer and essay questions, take time to reflect and think about your answers. Being able to answer the question accurately is the most important thing, but remember to adhere to the writing formula, and don't slack off in terms of grammar or spelling.

Use Your Resources and Review Everything

A multitude of resources are available to you for test preparation so take advantage of them. Here are some things to be mindful of that you can tap into:

- **Study guides and notes:** Be sure to review all of your notes and use any study guides provided to you by your instructor.
- **Study groups:** If you're working with study groups as recommended in Chapter 8, take some time to develop additional study guides and practice questions and to drill each other.
- **Practice exams:** Your textbooks may come with practice exams either within the book or on an accompanying course or text website. Your school may subscribe to online text banks or resource websites you can use for specific disciplines. If available, take advantage of any practice tests.
- **Review with your study aids:** Use the study aids we discussed in the last chapter, such as flashcards, to prepare. Review any concept maps you've developed to help you understand the bigger picture. These help tremendously with essay questions.
- **Work with your tutors:** Visit your tutoring center or program and work with tutors to review concepts to be sure you have things down. Tutors may be able to help you drill and prepare for exams if they tutor for the class or discipline you are enrolled in.

Whenever I reviewed for exams, my strategy was always to review notes and work with my study group, usually at an eatery near campus as an undergrad, or at the campus library or a Starbucks while in grad school. Good times!

Things to Understand

As you prepare for your tests and exams, be sure to understand the following: key terms and their definitions, key concepts, causes and effects, relationships and systems.

Fill in the Blank and Matching

When preparing for fill in the blank and matching questions, be sure you understand key words and their definitions.

Short Answer and Essay

When preparing for short answer and essay questions, you will need a thorough understanding of causes and effects or the basic facts of what you've learned so you can answer questions logically and thoroughly.

Be sure to *answer* the question! I've spent years reading student answers to short answer and essay questions where they never answer the actual question but provide information that dances around it, goes off on tangents, or is complete BS. Be sure to answer the actual question!

SUMMARY

In this chapter, we discussed how to prepare for tests and exams. Some of the strategies we discussed include anticipating the test questions, anticipating the question types, reviewing your notes and study guides, taking practice tests you have access to, preparing with your study groups and tutors, and using your learning aids.

Be sure to know key words and definitions and to be able to explain basic facts, key concepts, and causes and effects. Finally, when working with short answer and essay questions, be sure to answer the question, avoid tangents, and be mindful of your spelling and grammar.

> "Be prepared, work hard, and hope for a little luck. Recognize that the harder you work and the better prepared you are, the more luck you might have."
>
> — Ed Bradley

Your College and Life Roadmap

Let's take some time to practice some of the test-taking strategies we've discussed.

Exercise 1: Practice Tests

Find out whether your textbook has practice tests in it or on its publisher's website. Learn whether your college or campus learning resource center or library subscribes to online support services or databases that come with test banks for your class, subject matter, or discipline.

Exercise 2: Develop Your Own Practice Test

Working by yourself or with your study group, anticipate some of the questions you can expect on your next exam. Review your class notes or study guide, develop some questions, and drill yourself or your study group partners.

17

BRAINSTORMING—UNLOCKING YOUR MIND

"Think left and think right and think low and think high.
Oh, the thinks you can think up if only you try."

— Dr. Seuss

A Look Back, a Look Ahead

In the last chapter, I shared test preparation strategies and tips. In this chapter, we will take a look at brainstorming with a review of Chapter 14 where we talked about mind mapping.

What Does Brainstorming Have to Do with Life?

Throughout your life, you will always be called upon to generate ideas, come up with solutions, or nurture your creativity. Brainstorming is the process of generating ideas and solutions. Whether you need to solve a problem facing your organization or workgroup, or you need to think of a way out of a personal situation, or you want to engage your creative side to write a story or a song, brainstorming is something you'll need to tap into throughout your life.

When Would You Use Brainstorming in School?

As a student, you'll be called upon to brainstorm semi-regularly. Here are some examples:

- **Writing a paper:** I was first introduced to brainstorming in my freshman composition class. Our instructor taught us brainstorming and mind mapping as a way to generate ideas for writing our papers when we needed to find a topic. We further used brainstorming to generate ideas for the key points we needed to make in our papers as a form of a visual outline.

- **Research topics:** In addition to writing papers, you will likely need to think of research topics as you progress through your degree programs. College teaches you how to conduct a research study of some sort, but you will need to figure out an area or several areas to research as you progress through your program and take different classes. If you find yourself stuck in identifying a topic, brainstorming various topics can help you find areas you are interested in so you can make a decision on a specific topic you wish to study.

- **When "stuck":** We all get "stuck" on occasion. Brainstorming can assist you in getting yourself "unstuck." We'll explore this topic further in the next chapter when we discuss writer's block.

Let It Flow

The first rule of brainstorming is simply to "let it flow." There are no bad ideas or silly ideas. The main point of brainstorming is simply to get ideas. Write any and every idea down. You will evaluate each idea for its own merits later, once you get ideas down; then you can weed out ideas that will not work or are not feasible. Let everything come out and write everything down. Don't inhibit or limit yourself. Sometimes, the most whacky sounding ideas are the best because they are so out of the box. Let it flow!

Use a Mind Map

In Chapter 14, we discussed mind mapping. Mind mapping is a standard tool used for brainstorming. The advantage of mind mapping is its visual nature and its ability to help you rapidly generate ideas because of the branching nature where one train of thought leads to another, resulting in getting out many ideas quickly.

I wholeheartedly recommend using mind mapping as a standard tool for yourself. Mind mapping has been a part of my arsenal of tools for years, and it has always helped me to generate new ideas, whether I was trying to come up with solutions to problems, generate new courses or lectures, or develop new project ideas or solutions.

You can use a piece of paper or a whiteboard to develop a mind map, but personally, I use Inspiration software or Bubbl.us to generate my mind maps. I endorse both software products if you want a software solution.

SUMMARY

In this chapter, we looked at brainstorming as a tool to help you generate ideas for papers and projects or for outlining points for a paper or speech. Brainstorming can be used throughout your life in any situation where you need ideas, whether in the workplace, to solve a personal problem, or to work on a personal creative project. When brainstorming, the number one rule is simply to let everything flow. There are no bad ideas when you brainstorm. Once you get your ideas down, you can evaluate each one, discard those that are not feasible, and pursue the best idea you've come up with. Use a mind map to help your brainstorming process.

> "The way to get good ideas is to get lots of ideas and throw the bad ones away."
>
> — Linus Pauling

Your College and Life Roadmap

Brainstorming is a life skill and tool you'll use and revisit as a student and throughout your life. Let's practice brainstorming.

Exercise 1: Brainstorming Paper Topics and Points

- First, brainstorm five potential topics for your next paper. Then pick the best one.
- Now brainstorm four points you wish to cover in your paper.
- Next brainstorm three examples to illustrate your four points.

Exercise 2: Brainstorm Solutions to a Problem

Brainstorm five potential solutions to a problem you are facing or that is facing your community.

18

OVERCOMING WRITER'S BLOCK—WORDS JUST DON'T COME EASY

> "It's not the fear of writing that blocks people, it's fear of not writing well; something quite different."
>
> — Scott Berkun

A Look Back, a Look Ahead

In Chapter 17, we took a look at brainstorming to help you generate ideas for papers, research topics, and solutions to problems you are facing. We also reviewed mind mapping. In this chapter, we will apply what you've learned to solve a common problem you may run into while trying to complete writing assignments as a student—writer's block.

What Does Writer's Block Have to Do with Life?

You will be writing in some form or another for the rest of your life.

Many of the careers you pursue will require you to write reports or correspondence with colleagues, vendors, customers, or clients. If you are in a writing-intensive career where you are required to write reports, a good portion of your job will involve writing. Even if you pursue a less writing-intensive career, you will nonetheless be called upon and required to write, even if only for personal correspondence with family or friends. You will be writing for the rest of your life, but at times, you may encounter some form of writer's block where you are uncertain of what to say or how to say it. Tools to overcome writer's block will help you.

In this chapter, I will cover some tools to overcome writer's block with a callback to brainstorming and mind mapping as covered in Chapters 17 and 14 respectively.

Let It Flow

The very first principle of overcoming writer's block is simply to get things down on paper. Write anything and everything. Don't worry about it making sense; simply let your ideas come out. You can always revise and delete things later. Much like with brainstorming, the main thing is to get something out and down on paper.

Let Go of Perfectionism

We often psych ourselves out thinking things need to be perfect. Letting go of perfectionism is a key principle in life. Nothing is perfect, and nothing should be perfect on a first try. You want to put out your best product, but maintain a realistic expectation of what you are doing. It is better to write down something you can work with and improve upon than to fret and get nothing down. Don't stand in your own way.

Writer's Block Tips and Tools

To get past writer's block and "let it flow," here are some time-tested strategies.

Free Writing

The basic principle of free writing is simply to *write*. Write about anything and everything, and simply "let it flow." As you free write and get your ideas and words on paper, your writing will eventually focus into something more solid that you can work with and revise into a more polished piece. You need to start somewhere, though, so free write and let your words come out.

Mind Mapping

In the last chapter, I discussed brainstorming as a tool you can use to generate ideas when you have none or are stuck. Brainstorming is a time-tested tool to help us when we face writer's block or are just getting started with the writing process. Mind mapping is a time-tested tool we can use to enable the brainstorming process. With brainstorming, we can quickly generate ideas that can prompt us in our writing. If you find yourself not knowing what to write, take a break and pull out a sheet of paper or your mind mapping software to brainstorm topics or points.

Word Association

Word association is a similar tool to brainstorming that you can use when you face writer's block. I spent several years of my life performing improv comedy on the Honolulu comedy circuit, and word association games were one of the tools I used to develop scene topics and ideas to perform and act out.

As an idea-generating tool, word association is very effective and easy to use.

Here's how to use word association as a brainstorming tool:

1. Pick a word
2. Think of all the other words that come to mind when you think of that word.
3. Repeat the process until you have several words and ideas you can work with.
4. Write away.

SUMMARY

In this chapter, we discussed strategies to overcome writer's block. First and foremost, you want to get ideas written down on paper. Any and every idea is fair game because you need to start somewhere and have something to work with. Mentally, you'll want to let go of any need for perfectionism. Recognize that your first draft is not expected, by definition, to be perfect. Writing involves getting ideas down on paper first, and then you can refine your pieces. Use free writing, mind mapping, and word association to help yourself generate ideas and points you can write about. With ideas generated through free writing, mind mapping, and word association, you should have sufficient ideas you can use to get some writing done. Again, focus on getting ideas down. You can always go back and revise to polish and wordsmith your writing, add in additional points that come to mind, delete underdeveloped ideas that distract from your piece, or flesh out the underdeveloped ideas. Following these strategies can help you overcome writer's block.

> "First drafts don't have to be perfect.
> They just have to be written."
>
> — Author Unknown

Your College and Life Roadmap

Writing is a lifelong skill you will need to use throughout your life. Let's practice some of the skills we discussed to help you overcome writer's block.

Exercise 1: Free Write

Free write on a topic of your choice.

Exercise 2: Word Association

Use word association to help you generate ideas to write about, whether topics or points to support your topic.

19

PICKING RESEARCH TOPICS—BECAUSE YOU NEED TO

"Research is to see what everybody has seen, and to think what nobody else has thought."

— Albert Szent-Gyorgyi

A Look Back, a Look Ahead

In the last chapter, we talked about overcoming writer's block while revisiting brainstorming and mind mapping. In this chapter, I will continue with the writing theme and look at picking research topics, something you will need to do as a college student.

What Do Research Topics Have to Do with Life?

As humans, we all need to find information to answer questions or solve problems. Even after school, you will be called upon to research things, be it for personal interest or because you are assigned to do so in your career. While you may not become an academic researcher, you will need to learn how to ask pertinent questions and to know where to acquire the information you need to answer the questions you have, whether you are researching places to visit on vacation, or prices for airfare or car rental, or finding a good new place to eat that you haven't tried yet on a Friday night.

In this chapter, we will focus on picking good research topics for your classes. We'll also give special attention to developing areas of interest and expertise that you can leverage for your career or future schooling.

Tips on Choosing Research Topics

In picking research topics, I encourage you to be forward-thinking. I personally learned the importance of forward-thinking in grad school. Here are the three tips to keep in mind when thinking of research projects. We'll explore each in more depth below.

- Pick something that interests you
- Pick something relevant to your job or career that you can apply beyond the classroom
- Pick a topic that focuses on a relevant problem in your community, industry, or profession

Pick Something That Interests You

First and foremost, pick a topic you are sincerely interested in and, ideally, passionate about. You'll be spending quite a bit of time thinking about it, reading up on it, and collecting relevant data for it, so be sure it's something you're interested in learning about to justify the amount of time you'll be investing in it.

As an undergrad, I conducted two major research projects, one as a sophomore in a sociology class I took, and one for my senior thesis, which I spent an entire semester working on. For my sociology class, I chose to study youth incarceration. It was a topic my instructor suggested from a list of potential topics he gave out to our class. It was not something I would have thought of on my own, but out of all the topics, it was the one I was most interested in and passionate about for personal reasons since I came from a community with high crime rates among youths, which had personally affected some of my family members.

For my senior thesis, we had the luxury of choosing our own topics to research. I chose professional wrestling in a content analysis since it was a topic of deep personal interest to me. As a graduate business student, I revisited professional wrestling in a class I took on business strategy. I had looked at business strategies that smaller wrestling companies could employ to grow their market share, business, and bottom line in comparison to the industry leader.

Given my personal interest and passion for these areas, I was able to learn the academic skills required for my field while applying them to something I was interested in. My interest in the topic motivated me to do the study, and I came away with information I found of personal use.

Pick Something Relevant to Your Career

Think forward to your career and pick research topics relevant to it. When I returned to graduate school to pursue an education degree, for most of my projects, I conducted research I could immediately put to use in my job. I had the luxury of already working in my field so I could immediately use what I was learning from my research to improve my job performance and the organization where I worked. If you're not yet working in your prospective field, take the opportunity to conduct research for the job you wish to land. You will shine more impressively on your resume and may attract more job leads based on the research and work you've done because you can put it to immediate use solving problems in your field and bringing value to your potential employers. You will then stand out in the crowd of candidates. The research I conducted as an education graduate student allowed me to progress in my career and led to job promotion because the work I conducted was immediately applicable to problems my organization was facing.

Pick a Local Community Problem Relevant to Your Field

One final tip related to forward thinking is to conduct research on a problem facing your community that is relevant to your field of study. Research in its purest form is meant to solve problems and provide value to society. All professional researchers seek to solve problems. Unfortunately, a lot of academic research, in my experience, stays within academic circles or is conducted on narrow or niche fields that provide limited benefit. The true value of research, in my opinion, is to solve problems relevant to the communities where we live. I encourage you to conduct research in problem areas facing your community within the scope of your field of study. Doing so will put you in a position to work and contribute to your community, thus opening up job possibilities or creating business opportunities for yourself and the chance to be viewed as a community leader. We all want to better our lives and the lives of our families, friends, and neighborhoods. Take some time to conduct research that will directly impact your community if the results of your research are acted upon. You don't need to save the world, but you can definitely improve part of it. The world will be better off for your efforts.

In addition to these three guiding tips, don't forget to use the standard brainstorming and mind mapping techniques we discussed in Chapters 14 and 17.

Work with the Professionals

If you're having difficulty choosing or narrowing your research topic, consult with your instructor. Many professors will require you to do so as part of the course. Instructors often may provide a list of topics you can choose from.

Another resource is your research librarian. He or she will be an invaluable source in helping you find the material you need to learn about your topic.

Subject Area Expertise

If you plan on pursuing graduate school, earning a doctoral degree, or making academia your profession, you'll find it valuable to build up subject and topical expertise on areas of research interest that you can continue to research, write, and publish on as you continue your academic career. All academics have their personal areas of research interest, which allow them to publish multiple articles or books to demonstrate their expertise and build their careers, leading to job opportunities and career growth in or out of academia as teachers, researchers, or consultants. If you look at many academic publications, you will notice a trend of continued publication on the same topics, but with continued expansion of the topics and deeper focus into them, which allows researchers to become recognized experts in their fields. If you are serious about research or developing some expertise in a field, I encourage you to identify your interests and develop relevant questions you would like to answer that will guide your research throughout your undergraduate and graduate level careers and that you can leverage into further work in academia or applied research as a professional in your field. Development of your expertise will lead to career opportunities for you within organizations or the starting of your own consultancy practice.

SUMMARY

In this chapter, we discussed how to pick research topics. Aside from brainstorming to generate ideas for topics, you'll want to work with your instructors for guidance. Be forward thinking by choosing topics that can help you advance your career prospects and develop expertise in your field that you can leverage. Choose topics that interest you, are relevant to your career, or can assist in solving a problem facing your community. Doing so can position you as an expert and lead to career advancement and consulting opportunities. If you are graduate school bound, developing this level of expertise as an undergraduate will position you for a solid career in graduate school and academia as a subject matter expert.

> "Research is creating new knowledge."
>
> — Neil Armstrong

Your College and Life Roadmap

Identifying relevant research topics and questions to your field of study makes you a focused college student and positions you for career success as a subject matter expert. Let's practice identifying research topics.

1. Write down 3-5 topics that interest you.

2. Write down 3-5 topics relevant to your current or prospective career.

3. Write down 3-5 topics that focus on a problem currently facing your community.

20

AVOIDING PLAGIARISM— GIVING CREDIT WHERE IT'S DUE

*"When you have wit of your own,
it's a pleasure to credit other people for theirs."*

— Criss Jami

A Look Back, a Look Ahead

In the last chapter, I provided tips on generating research topics. In this chapter, we will continue with the research theme and examine how you can avoid plagiarism.

What Does Plagiarism Have to Do with Life?

In life, it is always important to give credit where it is due. No one likes to have his or her work stolen or borrowed without credit. While folks may not have bad intentions, simply borrowing works without giving credit to their originators or owners out of ignorance, it is important always to cite the original owner or originator of a work or idea. Beyond concerns of copyright, it is a basic professional courtesy to attribute the source of an idea or passage.

Going beyond proper courtesy, be aware that a lack of credit to a source can open you up to legal liability for copyright infringement, dismissal from a school, or termination from a job if you pass off someone else's original work or ideas as your own. Proper citations and credit for works are critical as a courtesy and as a means of limiting your liability and maintaining your personal and professional integrity.

What Is Plagiarism?

At its most basic, plagiarism is copying another person's work or ideas and passing it off as your own. In the digital age, it is very easy to copy another person's work through the simple act of copying and pasting something off of the Internet into your own Word document or Internet post. While copying and pasting information itself is not a crime, what becomes problematic is not citing where you got your information.

Plagiarism occurs when information is copied and represented as your own original thoughts, ideas, or works. Intentionally doing this is blatant theft of ideas or cheating. In the old days, this was known as copying someone else's paper, which most students knew was a form of cheating. In the digital age, where it is common practice simply to cut and paste information, many students may not be aware that they are cheating and stealing because everyone does so without a second thought.

Copying other works is usually okay, but you *must* properly cite any copied work or idea you've found elsewhere that is not your own.

Below is some general information on citations.

Proper Attribution and Citations

Giving credit to the originators of ideas, writings, or works that you use or pull from in your writings is called attribution or citation. At its most basic, when you cite or quote a work in your paper or research, you must provide the name of the individual or organization who wrote or published the work. In informal writing, it's possible to use quotes from others. At its most basic, if you don't know who said the quote, you would say something along the lines of, "A wise man once said..." because you know the quote is not your own and you do not wish to pass it off as such. If you know Thomas Jefferson originated the quote, you would say, "Thomas Jefferson once said..." This would be acceptable as a bare minimum citation because you've properly attributed a quote to an individual. In academic writing, though, you are expected to provide the "where" and the "when" of a quote, idea, or study you use. Revisiting our Thomas Jefferson example, you would cite the work as "In 1776, Thomas Jefferson wrote in the Declaration of Independence that...."

For academic writing, as a bare minimum, you always write the name of the original author, where he or she wrote the passage you are quoting, and the year he or she wrote it. Below are more uses and formats of citations.

Use Prescribed Citation Format

In academic writings, you are usually given a prescribed format for your citations according to the style guide used in your academic discipline. Three of the most common style guides used in academia are the APA, MLA, and Chicago/Turabian formats. Your instructors will typically tell you which style guide to use as part of the assignment instructions. Your programs will typically give you training in how to format your papers and citations in accordance with your discipline's style guide as an assignment or unit at some point in your program. If that is not done (highly unlikely), your school will provide resources and assistance in it, and the Internet also has a plethora of information.

Purchase the Style Guides

The best foolproof method to be sure you are properly citing your work is to purchase the official style guides for the publication style your discipline uses. Once you begin your academic major, you will learn which style your program uses. All of your classes from that point on will require you to write your papers in that particular format. The style guide will typically be a required textbook for your course or for the program. In the event it is not, it's a good idea to purchase a copy of the style guide book. In addition, it's a good idea to bookmark the official webpage for the publication style because websites publish any updates to the approved format as things change.

Work with Your Campus Resources and Staff

In addition to referring to the official style guides, if you need live support and assistance, be sure to work with your campus resources. Among the places you can go are:

- **Your instructor:** Your instructors are formal academics trained in research writing, so they know the citation formats inside and out. Ultimately, they are also the people giving you your grade.

- **Your research librarian:** Librarians are professional researchers trained in finding resources and citing them.

Often, campus libraries will host workshops on how to research and cite your sources.

- **Published resources by your campus library or learning resource center:** To assist student success, most libraries or learning assistance centers will offer research resources, including workshops or online guides on research and citations.

- **Writing tutors:** Your campus writing tutors are either professional staff or advanced students who are versed and knowledgeable about proper citation formats.

Summary

In this chapter, we talked about avoiding the unforgivable academic sin of plagiarism. Intentional plagiarism will get you an F grade in a course and you will be expelled from school. The challenge nowadays is many students may not be aware they are plagiarizing, given our copy-and-paste culture, so awareness is the key. Always attribute ideas and information to the source from which you got them to avoid plagiarism. Most courses will require you to adhere to a specific citation format based on the publication style manual of your discipline. Common publication style formats include APA, MLA, or Chicago/Turabian. Invest in a copy of the publication manual for your academic discipline's chosen publication format. Be sure to seek assistance from your instructors, librarians, or writing tutors if needed.

"For such kind of borrowing as this, if it be not bettered by the borrower, among good authors is accounted plagiary."

— John Milton

Your College and Life Roadmap

Avoiding plagiarism and citing your sources is critical as a college student. In the real world, being mindful of copyright can help you avoid legal litigation and keep you out of conflict with others. Let's explore how you can find assistance to help you avoid plagiarism.

1. Find official online resources for the major citation formats and style guides used by your classes and program.

2. See whether your campus provides assistance or online guides for research citations and style guides.

3. Find out whether your writing tutors on campus provide citation and style guide assistance.

21

LEVERAGING TECHNOLOGY— MAKE TECHNOLOGY WORK FOR YOU

"I'm a great believer that any tool that enhances communication has profound effects in terms of how people can learn from each other, and how they can achieve the kind of freedoms that they're interested in."

— Bill Gates

A Look Back, a Look Ahead

In the last chapter, we looked at how to avoid plagiarism and cite your works properly. In this chapter, we will focus on how you can leverage technology to make your studies and life easier.

What Does Leveraging Technology Have to Do with Life?

We are ever-increasingly a technology-based society. Technology permeates everything we do from how we communicate and how we get information to how we transact business. Being a savvy consumer of technology and adapting with the times as technology upgrades and improves will deeply impact your ability to compete and remain competitive for jobs and new business. In the meantime, being a tech savvy student will make your life—not just your studies—easier.

How Can Technology Help?

Depending on where you are in life, you may be a digital native who grew up with technology as second nature. Many of the things you'll read here may also be second nature to you, but it doesn't hurt to be reminded of resources you have available to make both your studies and your overall life easier. If you're a "digital immigrant" and are returning to school later in life, perhaps some of the information here will be new and valuable to you.

Whatever your past experiences with technology, it is an invaluable tool that will make your studies and life easier if you leverage it properly.

Throughout the previous section on college success skills, I talked in depth about various topics, including time management, note-taking, mind mapping, reading, writing, and other learning aids. I've informed you of some recommended software and technology resources at your disposal. In this chapter, I will give you a full overview of the type of software and devices you can use to manage your studies and life, and I will provide specific recommendations of products, most of which are free, that you can put to use.

It goes without saying that technology is very powerful. You can do almost anything with our current technologies. Here are some of the ways technology solutions can help you enhance your life:

- Writing your papers
- Preparing presentations
- Time and task management assistance
- Collaborative tools for group work
- Note-taking
- Study aid
- Dictionary and reference
- Learning aids for subject areas

Beyond assisting you with your school and learning needs, technology can also help you manage various aspects of your life. Here are some of the areas it can assist with:

- Money management
- Expense tracking
- Appointments
- To-Do lists
- Gas station finders
- Public transport routes and arrivals
- Ride sharing
- Food journal/calorie counting
- Exercise tracking
- Biometrics
- Medication management
- Communication
- Instant messaging
- Food and beverages

- Coupons (Groupon/Living Social)
- Happy Hour
- Starbucks
- Groceries
- Store apps
- Coupons/Rebates
- Entertainment

At the start of the smartphone and mobile application era, there was a mantra "There's an app for everything." As time has gone on, that has become true. Whatever you can think of or need assistance with in your life, somewhere out there is a technology solution. Education and learning assistance is one such area. Let's delve specifically into how you can leverage technology to power your learning!

Invest in a Smartphone

A smartphone is one of the best investments you can make to enhance your life and empower your access to technology resources. I highly recommend getting a smartphone. Finance it if you don't have the means to buy one outright. Most dealers offer student rates, so take advantage of that and get a great discount on your phone. If purchasing a new one is too costly, buy a good used one from a family or friend who is trading up, or if you're brave enough, buy a used one online.

Having access to mobile computing resources will be a *big* help in getting you the information and access to resources that you need.

Get a Laptop or Tablet

Perhaps the best technology investment you can make will be a good laptop or tablet device like an iPad, Kindle Fire, or Surface. Laptops and tablets give you the flexibility to access mobile computing resources on the go and are big enough for you to get practical work done on them such as writing your papers. With them, you can be productive on the go, be it in class, in the library, or at a coffee shop. A good mobile computer is the best investment you can make to empower your education. Finance a device if you don't have the immediate means to buy one.

As an undergrad, I didn't have the means to purchase a laptop, but I did have a computer at home that allowed me to accomplish all the work I needed to do. Years later, when I returned to grad school, I had a laptop in tow, and my access to mobile computing saw me successfully through the completion of three graduate degrees.

Recognizing the benefits of mobile computing, many colleges and high schools now invest significantly into offering students laptops as a recruiting and retention strategy. If your school doesn't offer one as an incentive and you don't already have one, definitely take the initiative to get one for yourself.

Once again, most technology manufacturers and dealers, including college bookstores, offer student discounts on laptops or tablets. Take advantage of the cheap rates to get yourself a good device. If even discounted devices are out of your means, see whether you can get a good used one off of a family or friend who is upgrading or purchase one online.

Getting a good computer is a key critical strategy for succeeding in college.

Use Campus Computing Resources

Just about all college campuses will have a computer lab available along with Wi-Fi hotspots. If you don't have the means to get a computer device for yourself, become familiar with where all the computer labs on campus are located and take advantage of those resources to get your work done for school.

Software You Need

Below is a list of software you should get access to. It will allow you to do most of the work required for your classes. If you are in a specialized major that requires special software, your instructors will share those requirements with you.

Whatever computing device you purchase, be sure you have access to the following types of software. I've provided examples of each in parentheses, and I'll share with you some recommendations in the next section.

- Word processor (Google Docs, Microsoft Word, Scrivener)
- Web browser (Chrome, Firefox, Safari, Internet Explorer)
- Presentation (Google Docs, PowerPoint, Keynote)
- Data Backup (Dropbox, One Drive)
- Calendar/Time Management (Google Calendar, Outlook)
- Task/To Do List (Google Calendar, Outlook)
- Note-taking (Evernote) or Audio Recording Software
- Research citation (Zotero)
- Collaborative Communication Software (for text messaging, instant messaging, group chat)
- Flashcard apps

With these items in your technology toolkit, you'll be able to complete most of the writing, research, note-taking, file management, time management, and communication tasks you'll need to do for your assignments and you can stay in touch with classmates and instructors.

Recommended Free Software/Apps

In this section, I will give my personal recommendations for software you should consider adopting if you have not done so yet. In most cases, I was among the beta test group for these products and have used them successfully in my graduate school and professional careers.

- **Email:** *Gmail* is by far the best email product on the market. You can access it off of a regular computer through a web browser or via mobile app on your mobile device. A chat messenger is also built into the app, allowing you real-time communication and collaboration with classmates.

- **Time management:** *Google Calendar* is my calendaring software of choice. It is conveniently packaged as part of the Google Apps suite alongside Gmail, and it is accessible from your computer via the web or mobile app device, syncing automatically.

- **Productivity suite:** *Google Docs/Drive or Office 365 or OpenOffice or Scrivener* for Word Processing. For your student work, you will need a word processor and presentation software at a bare minimum. Most office suites also come with spreadsheet software. The main products on the market are Microsoft Office 365, Google Drive, Apple's iWork, and Open Office. Depending on the computer you have, it will probably come with Microsoft Office 365 if you have a PC, or Apple iWork if you have a Mac. Google Drive is a freeware web app that comes with a Google account like Gmail. Microsoft Office 365 is free for students and the most developed product out of all the office suites. Based on adoption and usage in the professional industry, I recommend taking advantage of using Office 365 for free as a student but also taking the time to get to know and use Google Drive or OpenOffice because many organizations have chosen to adopt those platforms as a cost-saving measure. If you are a Mac user, iWork will serve you just fine, but I would recommend taking time to learn the basics of Office 365, Google Drive, or Open Office at some point if you are not already familiar with them.

- **Note-taking:** *Evernote* (Premium available to purchase). I was a first generation Evernote beta tester, and this software saw me through earning my Master's in Education and Master's in Public Administration degrees. I've been a happy user of Evernote since day one, and I haven't tried any other software since. Available as a freeware with paid premium features, Evernote is flexible as a desktop, web, and mobile app device and can also record audio notes.

- **File backup:** *Dropbox* (Premium available to purchase). I've been a happy Dropbox user since its beta phase, and while the product has had emergent competitors over the years, I have been happy with the service it has provided. During my undergraduate years, you had to take painstaking care to save copies of your work to floppy disks (no flash drives back then). When I got to grad school in the mid-2000s, we needed to save our work to flash drives or back up our computers to external drives to ensure we wouldn't lose our papers in the event our computers crashed. All of my data backup worries went away when Dropbox was released. As someone who suffered the trauma of losing a semester long project "back in the day" to a failed hard drive, I cannot stress the importance of having a backup system like Dropbox in place to ensure all your hard work does not disappear into the digital graveyard. With the ability to retrieve your files between multiple devices, Dropbox makes taking and updating your work on the go seamless.

- **Research:** *Zotero* or *Scrivener*. Research will be a *big* part of your college experience, and you'll need a good system to keep track of your articles and citations. Zotero is the best product on the market for organizing your research articles and inserting them into your papers in the proper citation formats per your required citation style. If you are a senior or graduate student, you will *love* this software. It saved me countless hours during my graduate years! Scrivener is a writing program that combines very elegantly the power of a word processor with a citation management system. Geared toward professional writers, Scrivener allows you to write any documents, be they short stories, books, screenplays, or academic works such as theses and dissertations.

- **Communication:** *Google Hangouts* or *Facebook Messenger* or *Facebook Group*. With the ability to IM or host video or audio conversations between individuals or small groups, Google Hangouts or Facebook Messenger are easily installed and used on your computer or smartphone. You may use them daily already to stay in touch with family or friends. They were mainstays in my graduate student experience. Setting up a Facebook Group for your clique of classmates is also a good strategy to stay in touch with them throughout your program and beyond.

SUMMARY

In this chapter, we reviewed why technology is important and why staying on top of it is a key success strategy for college and life. We discussed how you can leverage it to make not only your studies but your life easier. As a college student, you have the opportunity to purchase technology devices, software, and services at discount prices, so take advantage of your discounts—many of them free! Finally, I provided you with a list of recommended software for your technology toolkit.

> "The number one benefit of information technology is that it empowers people to do what they want to do. It lets people be creative. It lets people be productive. It lets people learn things they didn't think they could learn before and so in a sense it is all about potential."
>
> — Steve Ballmer

Your College and Life Roadmap

Using and staying on top of technology will get you ahead in college and in life. Let's get your technology toolkit set up!

Exercise 1: Get a Smartphone or Computer

- Shop around online for a good smartphone, laptop, and/or tablet.
- Check the websites of major manufacturers (Apple, Samsung, Dell, HP, Microsoft, Verizon, T-Mobile, AT&T, etc.), dealers (Best Buy), or your campus bookstore.
- See what the student rate deals are.

- Pick a phone or computer that meets the computing level you need.
- The more memory and processing power you purchase, the better, but there may be cost trade-offs.

Exercise 2: Software and Apps

Download, sign up for, or purchase the following software or software services:

- Browser (comes with your machine, but you may want to upgrade)
- Office Suite (Office 365, Google Drive, iWork, OpenOffice)
- Writing: Scrivener
- Email and IM service (Gmail)
- Calendar and To-Do (Google Calendar, Outlook, etc.)
- Cloud Backup Service for Data (Dropbox, One Drive, Google Drive, or comparable)
- Note-taking (Evernote)

Exercise 3: Apps to Study

Research apps that can help with the courses you are taking this semester. For example:

- Flashcard Apps
- Biology, Chemistry, Physics, Anatomy
- Algebra, Calculus
- Dictionary/Thesaurus

PART III
PEOPLE SKILLS

22

BUILDING RELATIONSHIPS WITH YOUR INSTRUCTORS

"Since we never get everything we want or need from our families, we look for sufficiency in surrogates."

— Richard Brookhiser,
Founders' Son: A Life of Abraham Lincoln

A Look Back, a Look Ahead

Up to this point, I've helped you kick-start your college career by teaching you how to navigate the college system. You've learned how to pick out your classes, find the right major, obtain financial aid, and learn about campus resources. We've also gone over various college and life success skills that will not only help you in your studies but your life as well. Now for the next two chapters, I will talk about another key college and life skill: relationship building.

What Does Building Relationships with Instructors Have to Do with Life?

A truth in life is and always will be "It's not what you know; it's who you know." Beyond that, a big part of your life success will be to learn from people who have paved the way for you. Throughout your life, you will meet many mentors who will help guide you throughout your career and life phases. Your professors are among the first mentors you will meet in your career. As with other mentors, they can impart their knowledge, experience, and wisdom to you and build valuable connections for you as you progress from school into your field. Knowing how to build and manage those relationships is an important skill you will need throughout your life.

In this chapter, I will provide some guidance on how you can cultivate and develop a positive professional relationship with your professors.

Why You Should Develop a Positive Relationship with Your Professors

Your professors, particularly those teaching your major courses, are invaluable resources to you. They have the wisdom, experience, and knowledge to help you enter into your field. Beyond that, they also often possess valuable connections for helping you land a job in your field post-graduation. College professors are respected members in your profession and employers often look to them for recommendations on good potential employees. Professors can often be your biggest advocates at this stage of your life. Whether you are applying for a scholarship, transferring from a junior college to a four-year college, applying to a graduate program, or applying for a job, your professors are your best source for references and letters of recommendation.

Beyond being good references, your professors may develop into your lifelong mentors, colleagues, and even, ultimately, friends. Personally, I graduated from my undergraduate program nearly twenty years ago, but to this day, I maintain a close professional relationship with one of my professors and regularly contact her. My graduate school professors are also regular colleagues I happily keep in contact with as part of my extended support network because we all work in the same field.

Over the years, I have been to many alumni recognition events and taken part in alumni recognition projects. I have heard many, many, many endearing stories from alumni about the treasured relationships they developed with their professors and counselors who helped them get a start in their careers.

Personally, I count many of the great teachers I had the privilege of studying under as blessings. They were major influences on the person I am today and the approach I've developed toward life, which has led to all of my success.

It is my hope that you, too, are able to develop these types of lifelong and collegial relationships with your instructors and that they provide you with the support you need to persist through your studies and enter your career field.

Be Easy to Work With

One of the best ways to build a good relationship with your instructor is simply to be easy to work with. No one enjoys working with someone who is a pain, whether it's because of an off-putting personality or high maintenance tendencies that create extra work. During my years working in the classroom, I can still remember my favorite students who were easy to work with and the students who were *not*. Here are the best ways to make a good impression by being easy to work with:

- Attend class punctually.
- Do the work assigned on time.
- Come prepared and ready to learn by asking good questions and making positive contributions in class.
- Have a good attitude by being pleasant and professional.
- Don't be a problem student or create extra work or headaches.

Professors love working with students, and most remember students who do the work on time, follow directions on assignments, and make relevant and insightful contributions to class discussions. They also remember students who show positive attitudes and have pleasant personalities.

Professors don't have fond memories of students who make unnecessary work with behavior issues or contentious personalities. As in other parts of life, no one likes working with someone who has a bad attitude or is high maintenance, nitpicky, a whiner, a complainer, never prepared, or doesn't do his or her share of the work.

Over the years, I have had students ask me for recommendation letters who should have known better than to ask. These students never did the work or never did it on time. Many of them had horrible attitudes. They received a resounding "No" from me. Conversely, whenever I got requests for recommendation letters from ace students, I had absolutely no qualms about writing them resounding endorsements for whatever job, scholarship, or program of study they were trying to get into.

Some of you may fall into the great middle of neither having been a horrible student who caused problems or not standing out as a rock star. That's perfectly fine. You may not necessarily earn a glowing recommendation, but you may earn a decent recommendation that definitely beats a one-star "would not recommend" or "avoid this person" review.

Building a Professional Relationship

Beyond simply attending classes, the best way to develop a relationship with your professors is to work with them outside of class. Class time is limited to just a few hours a week in environments where you are one of a large classroom of students. These environments are not conducive to forming particular bonds or meaningful relationships with people, so you will need to take time to work with your professor outside of class.

Visit During Office Hours for Assistance

As discussed in Chapter 6, all professors must maintain office hours to see students and offer help. This is your time to get one-on-one time and help with class material from them. It is also a good time to get to know them better. You will most likely interact with instructors teaching your major courses quite a bit since you may be taking multiple classes from them over time. This is where you have your best chance of getting to know them.

Share Your Professional Goals

Over the course of your program, identify the professors you most "click" with. You may find yourself taking most of your classes from a few of them, but like any human relationship, you may find yourself clicking more with certain ones because you hold similar views, share similar interests, have similar or complementary personalities, or have similar backgrounds. These professors will probably be the most supportive of your professional goals during and after your program. During office hours, take some time to share your goals with them. They may solicit this information from you during the program as part of your program advising or a class assignment. Regardless, as you get to know them, remind them of your goals so they will start to provide you with information and resources to lead you in the right direction.

Stay in Touch with Them

If you've built up enough of a relationship with your professor, be sure to stay in touch with him or her after the semester or after graduation. Professors *love* hearing from former students, provided you had a good relationship. Speaking for myself and most of my colleagues, one of the greatest joys we take as educators is seeing how well former students have prospered and blossomed in their lives long after leaving the classroom. Whether you send an email or a postcard to the college postal address, professors will feel that getting notes saying how you're doing in your new studies or career makes all the stress of teaching worthwhile. Also, if your school or program holds alumni functions, events, and reunions, attend them.

Social Media: LinkedIn contact

Social media is a contentious area in academia. A large debate exists about the separation of professional and personal spaces. That said, social media is, by far, the easiest way to stay connected to your professors, aside from their work emails, and many people are followers and friends with former professors on social media platforms. Therefore, I endorse connecting with your professors on LinkedIn if they have a LinkedIn profile since that social network is designed for professional contacts.

Your professors, by nature of your relationship, are part of your professional network.

As far as Twitter goes, it is an open platform (unless your professor made his or her Twitter account private), so if you're both Twitter users, in my opinion, it's relatively harmless and uncontroversial to follow someone there.

As for Facebook, I am friends with many former students on Facebook, and I have many colleagues who accept friend requests from former students. I am friends with many of my former professors on Facebook as well. I friended many of them while a student in their classes based on how well our relationship went (my program was very small and family-like). Given the intimacy of Facebook, though, I recommend holding off on friending your professors until you are no longer in their classes. Many programs embrace Facebook, and if your program has built in that type of dynamic where your professors are comfortable friending you, then by all means go for it. Some instructors, though, and many of you reading this as well, may feel more comfortable keeping personal and professional spaces separate.

Recommendation Letters

Once you've developed decent enough relationships with your professors and as needs arise, you may need to ask them for letters of recommendation, be it for a scholarship (your most likely need early in your academic career), for a transfer or graduate program, or for a job. Here are some tips for soliciting letters of recommendation:

- Ensure you're someone worth recommending in your view, meaning you're a good student who goes to class and does the work!

- Give professors adequate lead time to write recommendation letters given their workload, at least a two-week notice.

- Give them all the information they need, including the address to send the letter to if it's not going to you personally, and a stamp and an envelope.

- Follow up with them as the deadline nears if you've not heard back from them. Professors are human, so it may have fallen off their radar. At times, professors have forgotten, and as a result, support letters didn't arrive in time, leaving students in the lurch; therefore, a gentle reminder never hurts.

- Return the favor. Be sure to send them thank you notes. If you have time, write them return support letters if they are up for promotion or renewal of their teaching contracts. Favorable support letters from students go a long way in helping professors earn promotions.

SUMMARY

Life is about relationships. We all need each other to grow and thrive in life. Your professors have the potential to be lifelong friends, colleagues, and mentors when you enter their profession. Treat your professors as the start of your professional network as you enter your field.

To build positive relationships, first be a good student. Secondly, get to know your professors outside of the classroom setting. Visit them during office hours. Share your professional goals with them. Stay in contact with them via email, mail, alumni events, and social media like LinkedIn, both as a colleague and on a personal level. Finally, if they write you letters of recommendation, return the favor by writing them support letters to help advance their careers.

> "Better than a thousand days of diligent study
> is one day with a great teacher."
>
> — Japanese Proverb

Your College and Life Roadmap

Building a good professional relationship with your professors is an investment that will pay great dividends and impact your college and life success. Let's start building a good relationship with your professors!

Visit your professors during office hours. If you are in your major already, decide which of your professors you click with the most and share your professional goals with him or her.

23

BUILDING RELATIONSHIPS WITH YOUR CLASSMATES— LIFETIME COLLEAGUES AND FRIENDS

> "Having a college degree gave me the opportunity to be… well-rounded. Also, the people I met at the university, most of them are still my colleagues now. People I've known for years are all in the industry together."
>
> — Jon Secada

A Look Back, a Look Ahead

In the last chapter, we discussed the importance of developing solid professional relationships with your professors. In this chapter, we will discuss the equally important need to develop professional relationships with your classmates.

What Does Building Relationships with Classmates Have to Do with Life?

A successful career, as well as a successful life, is very much tied to your ability to develop quality relationships with people. You will continually meet new colleagues throughout your career. Your ability to thrive in the workplace and advance is related in large part to your ability to work well with your colleagues beyond just your ability to perform the actual job tasks and functions of your position. Your people and networking skills will help determine your ability to advance and find opportunities in your career.

Your classmates, particularly those in your major program, will be your colleagues and support network while in school and in the field. You may end up in the same workplaces and companies with many of them throughout your career, and they may help you acquire new positions by reference. Depending on how circumstances turn out, you may even be working for a former classmate at some point in the future.

In this chapter, I will provide some guidance on how best to cultivate relationships with your classmates.

Demonstrate Competence and Reliability

First and foremost, put forward your honest, best effort in your work and in any group work setting, whether it's a group assignment or an informal study group you form with your classmates. If you join student organizations and work together to put on student events, put forward your best effort. Always show your classmates that you are capable of performing at a professional level. If you work hard, you will develop a solid reputation that will follow you and be reflected in people's recollections of you.

Secondly, follow through on your commitments to your classmates and team members. If things come up that prevent you from completing your commitments, ask for assistance from your team and be upfront about any difficulties that happen, whether the assignment was beyond your ability or whether other situations come up in your life that prevent you from completing what you committed to.

Finally, be pleasant to work with. No one wants to work with a colleague with an off-putting attitude or disposition. No matter how great a worker you are, if you're unpleasant to be around or work with, people will not want to work with you, and if it is in their power, they will choose not to.

Support Each Other

The next major concept in developing strong relationships with your classmates is to support each other. Teamwork is all about support. In addition to doing your part of the work, teams ultimately watch each other's backs and pull for one another. Whether you're motivating and pulling for each other to get through your group project, the next exam, the next club project, or an event you are working on, be there to support your classmates as they are there to support you. Life happens to many of us during our schooling. Feel free to reach out to classmates in need, or if life happens, feel free to ask for help, and repay the favor as needed.

Be Sociable

A final step to developing strong relationships with your classmates is to get to know them outside of school. College is supposed to be one of the best times of your life. Many of you will definitely become sociable with your classmates, particularly if you are living on campus. If you are going to school at a commuter campus with no dorms, definitely take the time to hang out socially after classes, whether it's at a nearby bar or coffee house, or by engaging in social activities. In your post-college life, people are always more likely to help out a friend if jobs open up in the organizations they work for.

Most of you probably will do this regardless, but in addition to social activities outside of class, be sure to connect on social media with your classmates. Your personal social brand is the best way to show your classmates who you are as a person.

SUMMARY

In this chapter, we discussed how to develop your professional and personal relationships with your classmates. Your classmates will be career-long professional and personal contacts you'll be crisscrossing paths with as you go through your career. Many of you will work together in the workplace. Some of you may even end up working for each other. Your college years are your time to show your future colleagues that you are a reliable and competent worker and professional who gets the job done, pulls your own weight, is coachable, and is willing to work. Do your part on projects you are assigned or you agree to work on. Support each other in and out of the classroom as you go through your program. Finally, be pleasant and sociable. Many of your classmates will become lifelong friends and professional contacts. Put your best foot forward and earn their friendship and support.

"We came as strangers, became friends, and left as family."

— Author Unknown

Your College and Life Roadmap

Strong relationships with your classmates will boost your college and life success. Whether as study buddies helping each other with homework or folks whom you hit the clubs with on weekends, your classmates will be one of your biggest supports in school. And many of them will be your coworkers or colleagues in your professional network in the years ahead as you start and progress through your career. Let's get started knowing your classmates ASAP!

Initiate a social activity with your classmates.

PART IV
MONEY MANAGEMENT AS A STUDENT

24

LIVING ON A STUDENT BUDGET—DEVELOPING HEALTHY MONEY HABITS

"Financial peace isn't the acquisition of stuff. It's learning to live on less than you make, so you can give money back and have money to invest. You can't win until you do this."

— Dave Ramsey

A Look Back, a Look Ahead

So far in this book, we've talked about the skills for college success, cultivating good relationships with your classmates and professors, how to fund your education, picking your classes, identifying a good major, and finding campus services and learning resources to help you succeed. In this section, we will discuss a key skill you'll need to learn at this stage of your life that will carry you throughout the rest of your life: money management. If you can form good spending, saving, and money management habits now, you'll set yourself up for success in the years ahead.

What Does Money Management Have to Do with Life?

Managing your money is a critical life skill you'll need to have from now until the day you die. People run into money problems early because they do not learn to live within their means. They spend more than they earn. Learning to budget and live within your means coupled with saving habits will set you up for financial success throughout your life. College is the best time to learn these habits because you learn them when your earnings are less. You'll learn to value the money you do make so you'll appreciate it when you make more later in life.

Living on a Student Budget

As a young college student, your earnings are fairly minimal, if any. You may have the luxury of your parents subsidizing you so you do not need to work and can put all of your energy into your studies. Or you may be putting yourself through school by working jobs with low pay. If this latter scenario describes your situation, this section will help you to develop good money habits for the future. For those of you returning to school later in life, hopefully, it will make you aware of some additional cost savings areas and benefits.

Step 1: You Need a Budget

One of the most basic money management principles you'll need to formulate is developing and adhering to a budget.

> **What Is a Budget?**
>
> A budget is a list of where your money is coming from (your revenue) and where it is going (your expenses). I'll give you an example of some typical revenue and expense categories below.
>
> A budget is typically developed and tracked using a spreadsheet.

In the old days (before my time and yours), ledger sheets were used to develop these. Today, you can use a software program like Microsoft Excel to develop a spreadsheet to track a budget, or you can use various premade programs like Quicken or smartphone apps.

Budgets track your revenue and expenses on a monthly basis so you can develop a monthly budget. Since most people typically pay bills on a monthly cycle while earning money every two weeks in a job, it makes monthly budgeting fairly easy.

Why a Budget Is Important

Budgets are important because they give you a clear picture of your finances, including your commitments. They help you control your spending and make you aware of any potential money shortfalls you have. A budget is an estimate of what you expect to make and what you expect to spend over a period of time. While unexpected expenses may come up or you may not work as many hours as expected, a budget is still necessary to help you plan your spending.

Revenue

Revenue is your sources of income. Examples of revenue sources include:

- the paycheck from your job
- gifts from your parents
- money you make from side jobs, gigs, or business
- tuition assistance, financial aid, or scholarships

When setting up your budget, you'll want to add each of these as a revenue category if they are sources of revenue for you, and fill in the typical dollar amounts you earn in these categories.

Expenses

Expenses refer to all planned expenditures. Examples include:

- Rent
- Utilities (electric/cell phone/Internet/cable)
- Food
- Clothing
- Transportation
- Entertainment
- Tuition
- Gym membership
- Medical (doctors, prescriptions)
- Debt payments

When setting up your budget, you'll want to include each of these areas you spend in as a potential budget category; then allocate the typical dollar amounts you spend in each area.

One popular and highly recommended app for helping you with your budgeting is You Need A Budget (YNAB) which is available on the web, Android, and iOS.

Step 2: Control Your Spending

A key concept of money management that gets many folks into trouble is not controlling their spending. Consumer debt cripples the lives of many Americans because they spend much more than they earn. The ready availability of credit cards and our consumerism culture enables this. Many of our spending categories are relatively fixed, such as our rent and utilities, so those are difficult costs to cut, aside from finding cheaper housing or doing without things like cable or Internet service. It's cheaper to cut costs in categories such as food and entertainment, which is where most people expend their "disposable income" (what's left after paying for necessities).

In the next chapter, I'll share with you some money-saving tips and strategies.

Step 3: Increase Your Revenue

On the flip side of the equation, you can always try to increase your revenue. As a student, this may prove difficult because your time commitments may not allow you to take on another job, but here I'll outline the most common methods for earning extra cash while a college student. Personally, I earned money while in school by working on campus as a tutor and doing private tutoring gigs on the side. In the current economy, it's a lot easier than ever before to find and take on extra money-making opportunities. In the next chapter, I'll offer specific tips and strategies on how you can increase your income while a college student.

Step 4: Keep Track Of Your Money

Each day (or every other day), you should be logging your expenses or keeping track of them. You can use an app such as Mint or Quicken, which can link automatically to your bank accounts and also offer you cash spending tracking capabilities. Keeping tabs on your bank accounts and credit card limits will help keep you out of spending trouble (late fees, overdrafts, interest rates) and make you mindful of your spending habits. These apps help show you where your money goes and thus help you to make decisions on where you can cut spending. Both Mint and Quicken are available on the web, Android, and iOS.

Step 5: Start Saving and Investing

The final concept to apply to your life is the importance of saving. Even if you're not making much money, get into the habit of saving. You will want to open up a savings account at your local bank to set aside money for future short-term expenses. More importantly, you will want to open up a retirement savings account. While the idea of retiring may sound like a very far off concept if you're eighteen or in your early twenties, retirement accounts are among the easiest wealth-building instruments available. Even if you're just contributing $20 a month, start socking money away into a retirement account. At this stage in your life, you are probably not privy to a 401(k) or 403(b) or 457 account through an employer, but you are eligible to open an IRA if you have a job or a SEP-IRA if you are self-employed (Uber, Lyft, GrubHub, Instacart, DoorDash driver, Upwork, Freelancer, Fiverr, freelancer, singer, musician, actor, actress, dancer). Socking money away into both a regular savings account and a retirement account will put you in a strong financial position for your post-college life because you'll be that much closer to achieving bigger financial goals later, such as owning your own home. Your local bank may provide retirement account services to set you up with an IRA. My personal recommendation is to work with a company called Vanguard; it's reputed for having minimal fees and you can invest your IRA into a Target Retirement Fund account with Vanguard geared toward your retirement age. Another option that has taken off in recent years is the rise of automated mobile app based investing solutions such as Acorns, Stash, Betterment, and Robinhood. All of these apps allow you to invest into various investment instruments (typically funds) through your mobile device with the software recommending funds to you based on your risk tolerance, age, and financial goals. Check out each of these apps and services. Financial planning is beyond the scope of this book and my qualified area of expertise, but I recommend looking into some of these steps now with guidance from your parents and a qualified financial advisor.

SUMMARY

In this chapter, we took a look at how to live while on a student budget. We covered money management basics such as developing a budget, controlling your spending, ways to cut down expenses, ways to make extra money, how to take advantage of savings deals for college students, and the importance of socking money away into regular savings, retirement, and investment accounts to build toward your financial future. Developing good financial habits during your college years will set you up for a lifetime of prosperity.

> "The habit of saving is itself an education; it fosters every virtue, teaches self-denial, cultivates the sense of order, trains to forethought, and so broadens the mind."
>
> — T.T. Munger

Your College and Life Roadmap

Managing your money is a skill you will need to succeed in college and in life. Indeed, good money management is essential to your survival. Let's get you set up to manage your money soundly!

Exercise 1: Develop a Budget

1. Develop your budget on a blank sheet of paper or in a spreadsheet program.
2. Enter your revenue.
3. Enter your monthly expenses.
4. Are you overspending?
5. Where can you cut back on spending?
6. How can you increase your revenue?
7. Create an account on the web and download and install the You Need A Budget app to your mobile device. Then explore how it helps you with your budgeting.

Exercise 2: Track Your Spending

1. Track your spending for one month.
2. Keep all receipts and log them.
3. Use a spending tracker app on your phone, a spending tracker app on the web (e.g., Mint), a software program like Quicken, develop a spreadsheet using Microsoft Excel, or simply use paper and pencil.
4. Where is all your money going?
5. Where can you cut back on spending?
6. Create an account on the web or download and install Quicken to your mobile device. Play around with the software to see how it helps you better manage your spending and track your expenses.

Exercise 3: Check Out Investing Apps

1. Check out Acorns, Stash, Betterment, and Robinhood to see how you like each service and app.

2. Before signing up and officially investing, be sure to consult with a qualified financial advisor and planner.

Exercise 4: Open a Retirement Account

Find a qualified financial advisor in your community or ask at your bank to meet with someone in financial or investment services. Inquire about opening a retirement account for yourself.

25

MONEY SAVING AND MONEY-MAKING HACKS FOR THE COLLEGE STUDENT

"To understand someone, find out how he spends his money."

— Mason Cooley

A Look Back, a Look Ahead

In the last chapter, I shared with you the basic concepts of money management, including budgeting, what income and expenses are, and the need to save and invest your money. One of the key concepts I shared was the need to keep your expenses low and under what you bring in as income. In this chapter, I will offer specific tips and strategies on how to lower your monthly expenses and how you can increase your income.

Controlling Costs as a Student

If you're living on your own for the first time, learning to rein in your spending and find the best deals and money-saving opportunities is critically important. Fortunately, many time-tested tips are out there that I will share with you, including how to find food and entertainment deals, save on home furnishing purchases, and get the best coupons and rebates on your shopping.

Grocery Savings

After housing, your food and meals will be where most of your money goes (or should go). Everyone needs to eat. Typically, your choices are to eat out or to buy groceries and cook or prepare meals at home. Conventional wisdom suggests it is cheaper to purchase groceries and cook at home because you can often buy in bulk, prepare portions, and avoid the service and convenience costs associated with dining out. Here are some money-saving tips on grocery shopping:

- **Buy groceries in bulk and split the cost with your friends or roommates (assuming you have roommates and are living independently):** If you have access to shopping clubs like Costco or Sam's Club, you can save quite a bit on groceries by doing this. If this is not an option, join the shopper's club at your local grocery store and download the store app (if it has an app), or look at the local ads to keep tabs on deals.

- **Take advantage of coupons and rebates**. Newspapers always list ongoing sales at grocery stores and offer coupons for reduced pricing or rebates on common or manufacturer items. In this modern day and age, we are also fortunate to have many mobile apps that provide us with coupons or rebates when we shop at certain stores or purchase certain common items. I will share with you a comprehensive list of coupon, rebate, and discount apps later in this chapter.

Dining Out Savings

Dining out is a luxury. Yes, the food may be better and it is more convenient to have people cook your food and serve it to you. But convenience does come at a price. Still, there are many savings tips for dining out.

- **Pay attention to ads and window signs for deals.** Specials are often advertised on window signs outside of restaurants and occasionally in local newspapers.

- **Pay attention to local deal sites.** Specials are always offered on apps like Groupon and Living Social.

- **Follow local restaurants on social media.** Offers and deals are always posted on restaurants' Instagram, Facebook, or Twitter pages. Often, there are specific "social media deals" if you mention you saw the deal online.

A Word on Alcohol

Limit the consumption of alcohol: This is *extremely* difficult to do while in college because drinking and regular partying is part of the college culture, but while limiting it may not do much for your social life or status, it will help your bank account now and for years down the road. Alcohol is very expensive, can put a dent in your bank account, and limit your saving ability. Far worse, though, is developing an alcohol addiction that can lead to overspending, health issues, relationship problems with significant others or family members, and—worst-case scenario—legal troubles if you are caught driving or fighting while under the influence. Drinking can be a nice social activity, but it is best to drink responsibly and in moderation.

Retail Savings

Much like grocery shopping and dining out, retail savings are achieved through many of the same methods: paying attention to the newspapers, using coupon and rebate apps and sites, local deal apps, and following and paying attention to social media—especially if it's a local retailer.

Entertainment Savings

Entertainment refers to basically almost anything we do for fun, whether it's watching movies; going to plays, sporting events, or concerts; going out with friends to clubs; buying drinks; bowling; singing karaoke, etc. Activities like these bring a lot of fun and pleasure into our lives, but they also put huge dents into our bank accounts if not controlled. Here are some tips for cheaper entertainment when on a budget:

- **Take advantage of student deals for entertainment:** Many businesses in the community offer student rates or admission prices. Movie theaters, playhouses, clubs, sporting venues, and nightclubs offer student rates for discount admission or ticket prices.

- **Take advantage of streaming movies and TV shows online or via apps:** Cable subscriptions can be expensive, but services like Netflix or Hulu offer affordable plans to stream your favorite shows or movies. Many network channels allow you to stream their shows online or via app a few days after initial airings. If you like to watch movies the old way via DVD, Redbox offers a convenient and affordable option to rent movies while buying your groceries.

- **Borrow music and movies from your campus or public library:** Public libraries and many large universities have extensive collections of movies and music CDs available for you to borrow for free via your student ID or library card. Enjoy vintage entertainment for free at home.

Coupon, Rebate, Discount Codes, Local Deals

As mentioned in the sections on groceries, restaurants, and retailers, you can achieve significant savings through the use of coupons, rebates, discount codes, and local deals. Detailed below is a comprehensive list of popular websites or mobile apps you can use to find and earn rebates, coupons, discounts, and deals from popular stores, brands, and common products.

Cash Back or Trade for Gift Card Sites/Apps

- **Ebates:** Earn cash back for shopping online at most popular websites.

- **ReceiptHog (iOS, Android):** Scan your receipts to earn "coins" for trade-in for gift cards or PayPal cash.

- **ShopKick (iOS, Android):** Get points when you walk into a store or scan bar codes. Trade your points in for gift cards. Link your credit card to the app and get more points when you buy with your card.

Coupon or Rebate Websites or Apps

- **Ibotta (iOS, Android):** Cash back rebates on everyday

purchases from popular stores like Walmart, Target, Safeway, Sam's Club, Costco, Whole Foods, Kmart, Commissary (for military members and dependents). Earn rebates when you purchase certain items on the app.

- **Checkout51 (iOS, Android):** Cash back rebates on purchases for everyday items.
- **Find and Save (iOS, Android):** Earn rebates from popular stores with qualifying purchases.
- **GroceryIQ:** Organize your grocery and shopping lists and get manufacturer coupons for everyday grocery items.
- **SavingStar:** Earn digital coupons for popular grocery stores and drugstores. You can link your account to your store loyalty cards.

Discount Codes

- **RetailMeNot (iOS, Android):** Search for discount codes for purchases from websites to find the biggest savings for Internet shopping.

Local Deals

- Groupon
- Living Social
- Amazon Local

Furnishing Your Apartment

If you are living on your own and are in need of furnishing your apartment, there are two time-tested ways to save money on apartment furnishings, be they furniture or basic goods like pots, pans, plates, and silverware.

- **Visit a Thrift Store:** Thrift stores such as Goodwill, The Salvation Army, or Savers, and many other mom and pops offer bargain prices and used but still serviceable goods like tables, chairs, pots, pans, plates, silverware, lamps, etc. You can furnish your apartment on the cheap by shopping at thrift stores.

- **Bulk Day:** The old adage of "one man's rubbish" is one man's treasure applies even in this day and age. Many communities offer bulk rubbish pick up for families to put bulk items they no longer need on the curb such as beds, couches, chairs, television sets, and other items for city refuse workers to pick up. In many communities, you can time move-outs, be they at other colleges or military communities where people must clear out everything for a move in short time. Often, these areas become rife for the picking of "treasures" that are still usable because people must move out quickly due to expiring leases, end of semester, or if you're in the military, a Permanent Change of Station. "Treasure hunters" and "people on limited or no budgets" of all ages have used this method to score free deals on still serviceable items for ages. Whether you're looking for a bed mattress, couch, or refrigerator (you'll definitely want to Febreze these) or a good used TV, you can furnish your home FREE by taking in one man's rubbish and making it your own.

Transportation Savings

Everyone needs a way to get somewhere. Your options are either to take public transportation, hired transportation, or to drive yourself.

Here are some tips:

- **Public Transportation:** Public transportation is and always will be your most cost-effective mode of getting from A to B, especially if you purchase monthly passes for your local bus or rail system. Most public transit services offer student rates, and many have negotiated special rates with local colleges and universities to make public transit costs even cheaper for students.

- **Rideshare Services**: If public transportation cramps your style due to wait times, ridesharing services like Uber or Lyft are another option and can be made even cheaper if you split the cost of your bill with a friend or roommate, provided these services are available in your town. Sharing your invitation link also will help lower your bill as you earn ride credits toward your next ride.

- **Saving on Driving Costs**: The costs of owning a car and commuting daily can add up very quickly between car payments, gasoline, parking costs, and wear-and-tear maintenance. You can save on gasoline through apps such as Gas Buddy, which inform you of the nearest and cheapest gas stations. If paid parking costs are an issue for you, apps like Best Parking can help you find the cheapest rates.

Student Deals

As alluded to above, there are lots of financial perks to being a student. To recap, with a valid student ID, some of the savings advantages available to you include:

- Discount pricing on tickets at movie theatres, playhouses, concerts, and sporting events

- Public transportation: regular student rates and deep discount rates specially negotiated with specific schools
- Restaurants, bars, and clubs often offer meal discounts or student nights
- Technology: College bookstores, technology hardware stores and websites, and software companies often offer deep discounts to students for products like computers, laptops, pads, phones, software programs, and data plans. As a student, definitely take advantage of purchasing your tech products on the cheap.

Money-Making Tips

Working through college is nothing new. Not everyone has the luxury of a full scholarship or parents who can subsidize his or her studies. As I shared previously, during my college years I earned money as student tutor for my college as well as a private tutor. College students who work jobs at restaurants as bartenders, baristas, servers, hosts, or dishwashers; at retail stores as cashiers, shelf stockers, customer service, or sales floor staff; at hotels as counter staff, busboys; or as security guards at retail stores, shopping malls, and housing complexes throughout the community are nothing new. Fortunately, in this day and age of mobile apps and online marketplaces, your options for earning extra and flexible money are numerous. I share below some various recommendations on job options, ways to keep your tuition costs down, and flexible money opportunities.

- **Get a job on campus:** By far, this is the most convenient way to make money while a student, plus studies continue to show that students who work on campus while in school graduate in much higher proportions to their classmates who do not. If you need to make money while in school and don't already have a job, get a job on campus.

- **Keep applying for scholarships:** While you are in school, keep applying for as many scholarships as you can. They can help to defer your tuition costs, and books, supplies, and living expenses while you get your degree. You never have anything to lose by applying for scholarships other than the time it takes you to fill out the application and send in your materials.

- **Take on side gigs:** If you have a marketable skill, sell and market your services. You never know; doing so may evolve into a sustainable and profitable business that you can continue long-term. Post ads on Craigslist or search for available gigs there. If you're tech savvy or possess administrative, technical, and professional white collar skills, market yourself on Upwork or Freelancer for lucrative side gigs in programming, graphic design, video editing, audio composition, technical writing, editing, virtual assisting, accounting, social media marketing, or consulting. For small side gigs, offer your services on Fiverr.

- **Join the automated gig economy:** If you have a car, then driving part-time for Uber, Lyft, DoorDash, Instacart, or GrubHub is easy money because there is absolutely no marketing expense. If you don't have a car but you have a bike or don't mind walking, Postmates is another option for automated work or gigs as a courier. If you're not into driving and are handy with your hands, you can offer yourself for things such as household chores, house cleaning services, or home repair on services such as Handy or TaskRabbit.

Services such as these allow you to pick and choose your own hours at your convenience, allowing you to be your own boss.

> "The time making money should be greater
> than the time spending money."
>
> — Sophia Amoruso

Your College and Life Roadmap

Exercise 1: Find Out Student Price Benefits

Find out which products or services you can receive a discount or student rate for in your area:

- Transportation services

- Entertainment (movie, play, club, concert venues)

- Food and beverage (restaurants, bars, etc.)

Exercise 2: Download Rebate, Coupon, and Local Deal Apps

- Download the various apps we discussed such as Ebates, ReceiptHog, ShopKick, Ibotta, Checkout51, Find and Save, Grocery IQ, SavingStar, RetailMeNot, GroupOn, Living Social, Gas Buddy, and BestParking

Exercise 3: Technology Deals

Access to technology will tremendously aid your success in school and in life. If you don't have your own laptop, notebook, or smartphone, take advantage of the deals available to you as a student since you have special rates to products.

1. Check your college bookstore for its prices on computers, laptops, pads, and software.

2. Visit the Apple or Microsoft store in your town to see what deals it may have.

3. Visit the Verizon, AT&T, T-Mobile, or other wireless provider stores to see what deals are available.

4. Visit the websites of other technology retailers to see whether they offer special student pricing for products, software, or data plans.

Exercise 4: Freelance Yourself

- Check out websites such as Upwork, Freelancer, and Fiverr. Create a profile and consider listing any services you can offer with your special skills whether you're a good writer or good at accounting, programming/coding, graphics, video, audio, writing, or research.

Exercise 5: Drive People or Deliver Things

If you have a car, bike, scooter, or motorcycle and meet the age requirements, consider driving for services such as Uber, Lyft, DoorDash, GrubHub, Instacart, or Postmates if they are available in your town. You'll work as a rideshare driver taking people to the destinations they need or delivering things such as food, groceries, or parcels to people's homes, places of work, or businesses. Visit these services' websites and download the apps.

If you do choose to drive for Uber or Lyft, you're welcome to use my referral code for any ongoing sign-up bonus offers when you sign up through a friend. My referral codes are:

Uber: 7avf4qscue

Lyft: jonathan008938

Exercise 6: Help Out People With Their Chores

If you are handy or enjoy domestic work, see whether you'd enjoy making cash part-time via apps such as Handy or TaskRabbit if they are in your town. You'll help people with various things such as cleaning their homes, assembling their furniture, hanging things on walls, and moving items around or out of their houses.

PART V
FORTITUDE FOR SUCCESS

26

MASTERING YOUR EMOTIONS—EMOTIONAL INTELLIGENCE

"We cannot tell what may happen to us in the strange medley of life. But we can decide what happens in us—how we can take it, what we do with it—and that is what really counts in the end."

— Joseph Fort Newton

A Look Back, a Look Ahead

So far in this book, we've looked at identifying a career direction for yourself, finding the right school for you, funding your college and education, developing a variety of college success skills, managing your money as a student, and developing solid relationships with your classmates and your professors. In this section, we will take a look at developing the internal fortitude you need to manage the pressures of being a college student. In this chapter, we will specifically look at the skill of emotional intelligence, which includes how you can master your emotions so you can make clear decisions, maintain positive relationships, and avoid self-sabotaging behaviors that can impede your success.

What Does Emotional Intelligence Have to Do with Life?

As human beings, we are emotional creatures. As we all know from experience that sometimes we let our tempers get the better of ourselves. We may say things we don't really mean. We may not think through our actions or words, and then we end up doing or saying things we regret—even if we know better. Sometimes, we may let our fears hold us back so we don't take action when needed or we self-sabotage ourselves. Controlling our emotions rather than letting them control us is a critical college and life success skill. In this chapter, I'll provide an overview of emotional intelligence and share with you some tips on how you can keep your emotions in check so they don't get the better of you.

Emotional Intelligence

Emotional intelligence as a field of study has been influenced by the work of Daniel Goleman, who published the definitive book on the subject in 1995. In 2004, Peter Salovey and John Mavey published an updated model on emotional intelligence that has since added to our understanding and approach to this skill. If you would like to learn more about emotional intelligence beyond what is shared here, I highly encourage you to consult these definitive works. What I share with you here is my own synthesis of the material based on my experiences and observations on human behavior and knowledge.

Emotional intelligence is the ability to perceive, control, and evaluate our own and others' emotions. Based on our self-awareness of our emotions and our perception of the emotions of others, we are then able to control our emotions and our actions, behaviors, and interactions with ourselves and with others. Ultimately, emotional intelligence is the skill of controlling your emotions and not letting them control you.

How Our Emotions Undo Us

Our emotions are powerful things. If we are not careful with our emotions, they can get the better of us, limiting us from achieving success and damaging our relationships with others. Folks with poor emotional intelligence and poor emotional control often engage in self-sabotaging behaviors that hold them back, or they develop poor relationships with people due to emotional reactions that can put off people they want or need to deal with.

Here are the ways our emotions often undo us and thus hold us back:

- **Our Fears:** Fear is one of the most powerful emotions we face as human beings. Ultimately, our fears are what hold us back in life. Fears prevent us from pursuing the things we want or need to pursue. We often let them control us to our detriment.

- **The Past:** The failures of our past often control us, keeping us stuck in them. Many of us wind up "living in the past" and allowing what happened to dominate our fears, thus holding us back. Or if we do not develop more fears and anxieties based on the past, we may become trapped by our guilt, shame, or sadness over the past.

- **Our Guilt, Shame, Sadness:** Whatever happened in the past may trigger in us relentless feelings of guilt, shame, or sadness. We may blame ourselves for our past failures or

- **Our Anger:** Ultimately, much as Master Yoda of Star Wars fame teaches, "Fears lead to anger. Anger leads to hate." Our fears, guilt, shame, and sadness often trigger anger in us—anger at ourselves, anger at those we blame for our failings, or anger at our circumstances. We may allow our anger to consume us. Many times, we may act out of anger, damaging our relationships.

- **The Future:** Based on our fears, we may develop a bleak view of the future and get caught up in thinking that no matter what we do, the future will not be filled with success, but life will be a series of failures. Conversely, even if we do achieve success, we may view the future as having too many challenges that we do not wish to put ourselves through.

Whether through our fears, guilt, shame, sadness, or anger; our regrets over the past; or our anxieties about the future, we often let our emotions dominate and control us, paralyzing us from taking action or causing us to take the wrong action, and thus inhibiting our success.

Our Top Fears

Fear truly is a powerful, powerful emotion. At its worst, fear inhibits and controls us, stopping us from taking action and achieving our destiny. At its best, our fears can serve as motivation, pushing us to prove our inner naysayer wrong. Author, blogger, and career coach Bud Bilanich outlines a list of common fears that inhibit our successes:

- Fear of Failure
- Fear of Success
- Fear of Being Judged
- Fear of Rejection
- Fear of Expressing Your True Feelings
- Fear of the Unknown

In the next several sections, I'll share Bilanich's definitions and causes for each fear along with my thoughts on each.

Fear of Failure

Bilanich writes that the fear of failure is rooted in perfectionism and the false belief that everything you do needs to be perfect. Fear of failure is probably the most common failure out there. It prevents us from trying and undertaking things because we do not want to get hurt or discredited because of failure.

Fear of failure definitely held me back for years and still holds me back to this very day. The very first time I had to take an Incomplete in a course and earned an F for a class was my final semester in business school. During that term, life happened to me and I became very ill from a combination of work stress and stress in my personal life. I was unable to complete my classes and wound up in the hospital, so I did not graduate as I'd planned. It was the first time I'd ever not done well in school; up to that point, I had been nearly a straight A student, placing on Dean's Lists and Honor Rolls throughout my elementary school, middle school, high school, and undergraduate careers. For me, dropping and failing a class and not graduating as scheduled was one of the most devastating things that had ever happened to me. It was the first time I'd ever failed at anything I set out to do.

From that point on, I literally questioned everything I was doing both as a student and in my career. This fear of failure held me back for a long time, and it made me question whether I wanted to go forward in the direction my life was taking me or it was time to do something else.

After months of introspection and intensive therapy, I decided to get back in the saddle and try again. I did, in fact, complete my program, and over the course of the next several years, I went on to complete two additional master's degrees and entered a boom period in my career. The fear of failure was there for me at the outset after suffering such a major setback, but I went on to conquer that fear and proved my inner naysayer wrong.

Fear of Success

Bilanich also discusses how fear of success can hold us back in life. He says this fear is rooted in not wanting to take on the work involved with success as well as the fear of maintaining top level performance as a result of success. Counter-intuitively, while we all crave success, many people and organizations also legitimately fear achieving it. History shows many companies and celebrities who became "victims of their own success" because they were unable to keep up with or handle the pressures of the success they achieved. As many athletes or sports teams will attest, becoming a champion is often a lot easier than staying a champion. But that shouldn't necessarily stop you from trying.

Several years back, our college took on a new initiative to improve our students' retention and success. We initiated a pilot program that received great student feedback and demonstrated measurable results in the students' performance. The project was a success, but we faced a problem trying to sustain it. Many on campus were concerned about our lack of capacity to expand and support the program, given staffing and budgetary limitations. While the program was successful, many feared it could be the victim of its own success since we didn't have the means to sustain it. Business school case studies are also full of examples of companies that were wildly successful at the outset but ultimately undone because they could not meet expansion and demand.

In my opinion, you should strive to be a success, but if fear of success holds you back, plan on how you can handle and sustain your success or grow it incrementally to be sustainable. Managed growth is important.

Fear of Being Judged

Bilanich writes that fear of being judged is rooted in our need for others' approval. I agree that we are all conditioned to seek positive reinforcement from others from a young age, whether by seeking the approval of our parents and elders or that of our classmates on the elementary school playground.

In college, we are constantly being judged. We submit our work to our professors for grading and feedback. In our classes, we are often asked to share our work in front of others. Many times when we are assigned to do group work, our performance in a group setting may be informally judged by our classmates or formally judged because we are required to rate each other as part of the grading process.

In the professional world, we are also similarly judged by our bosses in our performance reviews and by our coworkers. Whether we like it or not, we are always being judged, evaluated, and assessed for our performance.

Part of overcoming the fear of being judged is always to keep the feedback you receive from instructors, bosses, classmates, or colleagues in perspective for what it is. I'll address this later in the chapter.

Fear of Rejection

Related to our fear of being judged is our fear of rejection. Bilanich shares that this fear is rooted in personalizing what people say about you or even do to you. We all have a need to be accepted by others, so being rejected is a very powerful fear. Anyone who has ever dated or job hunted knows how painful rejection can feel. Academia is no different when programs you apply for deny you admission or when an assignment you've poured your time, blood, sweat, tears, heart, and soul into comes back to you with a bad grade. The rejection can be crushing and demoralizing.

Much like the fear of being judged, part of overcoming this fear is keeping the feedback you receive in perspective. Again, I'll address this later.

Fear of Expressing Your True Feelings

Bilanich writes that this fear is rooted in fears of rejection or judgment of what you honestly feel. I extend this definition to being rooted in not wanting to hurt others' feelings. For example, perhaps you are writing a potentially controversial paper expressing new views on a topic that others may not have taken into consideration. This situation is fairly common in academia where we are asked to challenge conventional thoughts or explore different views to expand our knowledge and perspective. Many of us may have fears that others in the field will outright reject, criticize, or perhaps even mock our work. Such fear may prevent you from publishing or putting forward your work.

Conversely, you may have criticisms about someone else or his or her work, but not wanting to hurt the person's feelings, you keep your opinions to yourself. Doing so also inhibits you from expressing your true feelings.

Beyond academia, this fear may hold you back in personal relationships. You may choose not to express your feelings to someone you wish to explore a relationship with out of fear. You may choose not to write a short story, poem, or song for that person that you've been meaning to. You may choose not to provide loved ones or friends the critical feedback they need to hear to better themselves.

Fear of expressing your true feelings can potentially hold you back from taking action to change your career or personal life for the better.

Fear of the Unknown

Bilanich shares that fear of the unknown is rooted in the belief that "Everything bad that can happen will happen." Along with the fear of failure, the fear of the unknown can severely hamper us from "doing."

Explorers throughout history have always ventured into the unknown, whether it was across the desert, across the seas, or into outer space. Pioneers into new frontiers have been met with admiration for their courage to get out of their comfort zones and forge the way for us. Pioneers overcome their fears of potential death to expand our known horizons. Inventors and technology pioneers equally venture into the unknown, pushing the boundaries of what our technology can do for us. While their physical lives may not necessarily be in danger, many put their reputations or financial fortunes at stake. Fear of the unknown, in many ways, is related to the fear of failure.

In terms of your college success journey, you are fortunate that college is not an "unknown." Millions of students have successfully completed college before you. You have the benefit of not going into uncharted territory. You do, however, face the challenge of what is unknown to you. Can you replicate the success that others have had in your life?

Like anything else in life, success in college will require hard work on your part and following the examples of those who came before you. You will need to build and surround yourself with the support structures and system you need. It may be unknown territory for you, but you have the benefit of the experience, guideposts, and directions of those who came before you to help you find your way. Therefore, your fear of failure is what you will need to overcome.

Our Self-Sabotaging Actions

When we surrender to our fears and other emotions, we often engage in self-sabotaging actions that impede our potential for success. In this section, I will discuss these self-sabotaging behaviors and actions.

Avoidance of Action

The most common reaction we have to our fears and resulting emotions is avoidance of action. We cannot make a decision on what to do, or we simply choose to throw in the towel. Typically, avoidance of action manifests in one of two ways:

1. Procrastination

2. Completely blowing things off

We may choose to put off the things we need to do or know we should do. Procrastination hurts us because by waiting, we may delay the potential rewards we would have received had we acted earlier. Worse yet, we may completely miss our opportunity for reward by waiting, thus fulfilling our own prophecy that "Things would not have worked out." Equally detrimental is completely blowing things off, again fulfilling our self-prophecy that "Things would not have worked out."

Taking Things Personally

Related to our fears of rejection and being judged is our reaction of taking things personally. We may automatically view any criticism we receive or any perceived snub from others as an affront. We come to believe that people don't like us, are out to get us, think we are a bad or incompetent person, or any other number of negative traits. We take things personally as attacks against us. The danger here is that many times it is simply not true that others are "against us." Criticisms may simply be that—criticisms and not attacks. Some of our critics may not be our fans or supporters, but by and large, those who criticize us may, in fact, be our biggest supporters and simply voice criticisms because they want us to improve and be better. Criticisms from your professors typically fall into this category. Professors usually have no ulterior motive in giving "negative" feedback because they have no reason to "hold you down" or to believe you are a bad person. A professor's sole function is to teach you and work with you so you are prepared for the future. Taking constructive feedback from professors personally is counterproductive.

Feedback from classmates or colleagues about your performance in group settings is equally typically meant in a constructive format. While some of your classmates may have styles or personalities that clash with yours, most feedback done in a group setting is, ultimately, meant to make the group function better or optimally. Group members need to learn to function with each other, despite any challenges or differences people present. Feedback on the work you do or the way you do it is usually intended to accommodate discrepancies in work styles that impact the way the group performs as a whole. They are rarely meant as personal attacks. Ultimately, there's little need to take these criticisms personally.

Being Defensive over Criticism

Sometimes, taking criticism personally manifests into defensiveness. At its worst, it manifests in small arguments or tense conversations with or against your critics, be they your professor or a classmate. This defensiveness stems from your anger and hurt at being judged or rejected. Defensiveness can damage your reputation and strain your relationships with classmates, colleagues, professors, and other superiors. People rarely enjoy working with someone who is unable to take criticism in stride.

Blowing Up at Others

At defensiveness' worst level, you may actually blow up at people who criticize you and your work. Rather than getting into heated arguments, I encourage you to revisit and work to control your emotions. Getting into arguments with others will severely damage your reputation and your relationships. At its worst, it will open you up to disciplinary action. Beyond that, you will develop a reputation as an unprofessional person who cannot handle constructive criticism or take it in stride. As a result, people will be reluctant to work with you, once again fulfilling a self-made prophecy that folks are out to get you.

Beating Yourself Up

Just as equally destructive as taking out your anger on your critics is choosing to internalize your criticism and beat yourself up, believing you are not worthy, competent, or any host of other negative thoughts or emotions about your worth or your work. Unchecked thoughts such as these will begin to reflect in your performance and confidence. While not as destructive to your relationships, internal conflict with yourself will defeat you if you don't regain control of your thoughts.

Our Guilt, Shame, and Sorrow

If our fears remain unchecked and affect our performance, we stand the risk of becoming trapped in the past and becoming prisoners to our guilt, shame, and sorrows. These emotions can equally enable our inaction. Here are some common causes of guilt, shame, and sorrow:

- **Not performing to our own standard:** We may begin to beat ourselves up for not performing at the level we wanted or thought we could. Sometimes, we simply are unable to perform at the standard we are used to performing at for whatever reason. That's no reason to beat ourselves up. Conversely, sometimes our standards are simply unrealistic. Many people set such high standards for themselves that no one could reasonably achieve that level of performance.

- **Not performing to our parents' standard:** Many of us may start to beat ourselves up if we are unable to meet our parents' performance standards. I sometimes suffered from this. If I brought home Bs or A- grades, occasionally my parents would get on my case about why I didn't get an A or an A+. Much like with your own self-set standards, sometimes despite your best efforts, you didn't hit the higher standard. There's actually nothing wrong with that. Or perhaps your parents simply are setting unrealistic standards so you need to block out those standards, accept your level of performance, and seek to do better without putting too much pressure on yourself.

- **Not trying our best or not doing our best:** Sometimes, you know you've slacked off and not achieved your best and it bothers you. Sometimes, it bothers you so much that it eats you up and you beat yourself up as a slacker. The main point is that you know you slacked off and you know better, so pledge to do better next time. Working to improve yourself is much more constructive than beating yourself up over a past failure.

- **Not doing our part in a group**: Sometimes when you are assigned group work, you are not able to pull your weight. Perhaps life happens and you're too tapped out with other commitments that your commitment to the group goes unfulfilled. Or perhaps you simply lack the skill to contribute at an equal level. There have been times when that was true for me. All I could do was be honest with my teammates about my situation and my shortcomings and do my best to pull whatever weight I could; then I had to be satisfied with knowing that I had done the best I could with what I had.

Conversely, there were times when I knew I could perform better in my group but did not. At that stage, all I could do was accept that I underperformed when I was capable of doing better, apologize for dropping the ball, and work to do better in the future.

Beating ourselves up over and over is simply counterproductive. Les Brown sums it up best: "Self-pity is our worst enemy and if we yield to it, we can never do anything wise in this world."

Our Anger

Fears and negative emotions at some point lead to anger. In previous sections, we talked about the detrimental effects of our anger manifesting in outward displays at our classmates and others through arguments or in self-loathing. All are detrimental, whether in our relationships with our classmates or to our self-esteem. Here are ways our anger may manifest:

- **At ourselves:** We may develop self-loathing. The effects of self-loathing can be disastrous to our mental health, resulting in depression or other self-destructive behaviors like procrastination, due to our fear of failure, rejection, or judgment by others.

- **At our critics:** We may become angry at any comments we receive as feedback from our professors or classmates in regards to our assignments, performance, or contributions to group efforts. We'll see these comments and feedback as personal attacks against our character or competence, leading us potentially to arguments with our critics. These arguments could result in the blame game, where we start to find faults in their performance or characters, or where we attribute our failings to them or to others. While your critiques may be equally valid, it is important to acknowledge and own any feedback received, to do your best to keep any arguments professional, and to avoid personal attacks. No one will want to work with someone unable to accept constructive criticism or who devolves into confrontational, argumentative, or personal attacks when criticized.

Mastering Our Emotions

Ultimately, our goal is to master our emotions. In this final section, I will share with you basic strategies to master your emotions and utilize emotional intelligence.

- **Overcome fears through action:** Michel de Montaigne once said, "He who fears he will suffer, already suffers from fear." When fear gets a grip on you, the best way to work around it is simply to take action. Fears often stop you from doing what you know needs to be done. Work to overcome your fears by simply getting out and doing what you know you need to do. As Dale Carnegie said, "You can conquer almost any fear if you will only make up your mind to do so. For remember, fear doesn't exist anywhere except in the mind."

- **Let go of what happened in the past:** Often, we become stuck in the past, thereby losing our happiness in the present and the will to manifest the future we deserve. Seventeenth century Spanish writer Quevedo eloquently encapsulated this when he said, "He who spends time regretting the past loses the present and risks the future." One of life's truths is that it is best to make peace with the fact that the past is the past because there is no way to change it. What's done is done. You do have control over what happens in the here and now, and you can influence what happens in the future. Ultimately, if you feel you've screwed up in the past, simply learn to forgive yourself, move on, and use the past as the learning experience it is meant to be. As Paul Boese said, "Forgiveness does not change the past, but it does enlarge the future."

- **Accept criticism as a way to grow and improve:** Always take criticism in stride. People usually offer it as a means to help you. In the case of your professors, this is always the case. In terms of classmates, it is usually done as a means of facilitating a better working relationship with you. Inspirational author Norman Vincent Peale puts it best: "Never react emotionally to criticism. Analyze yourself to determine whether it is justified. If it is, correct yourself. Otherwise, go on about your business."

- **Control and let go of your anger:** Buddha said, "Holding on to anger is like grasping a hot coal with the intent of throwing it at someone else: you are the one who gets burned." Anger is simply a poison both to yourself and to those around you. The sooner you learn to let things go, the better off you will be. Every second you spend holding on to anger is one second less of happiness in your life. When you hold on to anger, it festers within you, and often, you wind up taking it out on those around you. No one likes being around or working with an angry or grumpy person. Emotions like that are a cancer. Learn to let go of whatever is angering you. If it is something you have control over, work to resolve it. If it is something that happened in the past or that you have no control over, just let it go.

- **Work to improve your communication with others:** Often, the sources of our frustrations or conflicts in life boil down to poor communication or miscommunication with others. Sometimes, we misinterpret things people say or do (fear of being judged), and in reaction, we say or do things that come out wrong or that we regret. Using emotional intelligence can help improve your communication.

- **Listen to others. Understand where they are coming from and tailor your response to assuage any of their fears:** At its highest level, emotional intelligence isn't just having insight into and controlling your emotions. It is equally the skill of understanding other people's emotions, thereby allowing you to process where the other person is coming from so you can communicate better and come to a happier resolution than when emotions take over. Work on listening without judgment of others or interjecting your own emotions into a conflict; instead, actually "hear" what the other party is saying and work to resolve things.

- **Say what needs to be said:** Many times, our fear of expressing our true feelings holds us back, keeping us in a position we don't want to be in. Learn to say what's on your mind and in your heart. Sometimes, being honest may put you into conflict with others, but the price you may pay is not being at peace with your true self for the sake of not rocking the boat. Often, your fear of not speaking up may be unfounded and you need to speak to improve a situation. Sometimes, situations may initially get worse before they get better, but in the end, it is worth it.

SUMMARY

In this chapter, we took a look at emotional intelligence. Emotional intelligence is our ability to control our emotions so we can take appropriate action when needed. Overreacting can set us back. Conversely, failing to act when action is needed because we are dominated by our fears can be just as negative. Emotional intelligence allows us to work through and process our feelings so we can take the right actions when needed. Often, regrets over our past may incapacitate our ability to function fully in the present, thereby holding us back from the future we are capable of. Learning to let go of the past is critical to our success. Our emotional intelligence is crucial to both our college and life success.

> "The sign of an intelligent people is their ability to control emotions by the application of reason."
>
> — Marya Mannes

YOUR COLLEGE AND LIFE ROADMAP

Emotional intelligence, the ability to control our emotions and to read those of others, is a critical skill. Overreacting to what people say or do can adversely affect our relationships and reputation. At the same time, surrendering to gripping fear or wallowing in self-pity that keeps us from taking action can make us miss opportunities in life. Let's practice and develop our emotional intelligence.

Exercise 1: Releasing Fear

What are some of your biggest fears that hold you back from pursuing what you want to achieve? Name these fears and what they are holding you back from doing.

Now take some time to plan how you can pursue at least one of these goals.

Exercise 2: Letting Go of Your Past

Are there things in your past as a student that you regret doing or not doing? Do these regrets hold you back in the present? If so, take some time to make peace with them and let them go. Light a candle or take a shower and let them symbolically burn or wash away.

In your personal life, are there similar events you have regrets over? Things you did? Things you did not do? Let these burn with your candle or wash away in your bath as well. By doing so, you are making peace with your past, liberating your present, and opening up your future.

Exercise 3: Accepting Criticism

Think of a common criticism about yourself that others have shared with you. Is the criticism valid? What can you do with that feedback?

The next time your professor offers a critique on your work, thank him or her for the feedback.

Exercise 4: Authentic Words

Are there things you have held yourself back from saying to someone? Are there new ideas or thoughts you've been meaning to share with the world? Take the time to voice these opinions and ideas and find your voice. Weigh your fear of negative consequences against the consequences of your silence. You will probably find that the consequences in your mind do not measure up to the consequences of bottling up what is inside of you.

27

MANAGING YOUR STRESS—IT'S A KILLER

"The greatest weapon against stress is our ability to choose one thought over another."

— William James

A Look Back, a Look Ahead

In the last chapter, we took a look at developing emotional intelligence as a means to help you create the necessary fortitude you need to survive college, the feedback and criticism you'll receive, and the personalities you'll encounter. In this chapter, we will explore another critical area where you'll need to develop fortitude: stress management.

What Does Managing Stress Have to Do with Life?

Throughout life, we will continuously need to deal with stressful situations. As you age and are required to take on more responsibilities, be it in the workplace as you advance in your career or through the responsibilities of raising children or caring for elderly loved ones, you will be stretched and tested to manage the stresses of life. Learning good stress-management techniques is a critical life skill. In this chapter, I will share with you some stress management techniques you can apply to your collegiate career, which you'll be able to translate and use throughout your life.

Stress

Perhaps the best place to begin is by simply defining stress. According to Webster's Dictionary, stress is "a state of mental or emotional strain or tension resulting from adverse or very demanding circumstances." Our lives have no shortage of such adverse or demanding circumstances. Let's take a look at some of the stressors we face daily.

Stressors
As humans, we all face common stressors in our lives. As a student, you face additional stressors based on the requirements you must meet as a student. Here are some common stressors faced by college students and people in general:

- **School stressors**: As a student, you face the stressors of meeting deadlines on your readings, papers, research projects, or group projects. You also face the pressure of earning the grades you need to move on to the next course or simply to pass. Some of these challenges can be quite stressful if you are in a highly competitive program.

- **Daily stressors:** Many of us face the daily stressors associated with life, including earning enough money to pay rent and buy groceries, fighting daily traffic jams, dealing with late or packed buses or trains, losing a wallet or cell phone, and getting kids to school on time. There are no shortage of daily stressors in our lives.

- **Life changes:** Sometimes, life happens and causes us to face major life stressors. A loved one in our family may pass away. We may undergo a divorce. We may be forced to move homes after being evicted or a lease not being renewed.

- **Workplace stressors:** Many of us will need to work a job or two while in school to pay our bills. We may need to maintain or meet productivity schedules or quotes depending on our jobs. We may also be forced to work with toxic coworkers who adversely affect our mental health.

- **Social and Family stressors:** Our social and family lives come with their own sets of stressors. We may be raising families or being tasked as caregivers for elderly or ill relatives. We may be responsible for feeding, tending to, and getting family members to school, games, activities, or doctors' appointments. Some of us may face social pressures to go out with friends for nights out or social activities. Many of us may face domestic violence situations with a significant other or abusive parent.

Whatever your situation, there is no lack of stressors you can be exposed to.

Stress and Control

When we face stressful situations, we can basically do two things: change the situation, or change the way we react to it.

Some stressful situations we can change while others are out of our control, but we can still choose how we handle and react to the situation.

In all situations, we always retain full control over how we react. Our ability to discern what we have control over versus what we don't is a valuable life skill. Knowing that you control your reactions to the challenges you face will empower you.

Stress Management

To manage your stress, rely on the following principles:

1. Do not overcommit yourself.
2. Know your stressors.
3. Tap into your support system.
4. Adjust your thinking.
5. Keep things in perspective.
6. Manage your expectations.
7. Get adequate exercise.
8. Find relaxing activities.
9. Get enough sleep.

I will examine each of these in more depth in the following sections.

Do Not Overcommit Yourself

One of the biggest causes of stress is having too much to do. If you find yourself overly stressed, ask yourself whether you are overcommitted. If the answer is yes, you'll want to delegate, defer, or decline some of your responsibilities as outlined in the earlier chapter on time management.

Take some time to reexamine the commitments in the various parts of your life:

- School
- Job or Career
- Family (Parents/Elders, Significant Other, Children)
- Social Life (Friends, Significant Other)
- Self-Care (Exercise, Hobbies)

If you find yourself overcommitted, see what things you can delegate in your work or family life. See what things you can defer in your work, family, or school life. Many deadlines are negotiable if you're willing to ask. People typically are willing to accommodate and work with you if you are facing extenuating circumstances. You simply need to ask. Finally, you may need to learn to say "No," or decline new requests and simply let people know you are too overtaxed at the moment.

Know Your Stressors

One part of stress management is to know what your stressors are. This knowledge will allow you to manage your stress better by either allowing you to work around and avoid these situations or, if unavoidable, prepare you to cope better with them. When you get overly stressed or are prone to anxiety, note what is the exact cause of your distress. Is it certain activities? Is it certain people? Is it certain places? Is it certain situations? Note all the stressors in your life. For the stressors you can control, what can you do differently to change the situation? For the stressors you have no control over, how can you react differently to help you better cope with these stressors?

Tap into Your Support System

The next major strategy to help you manage your stress is to tap into your support system. Your support system can provide you valuable resources to cope with stressors, or at the very least, lend an ear and be your cheering section. Whatever stressors are ailing you—be it lack of cash, lack of food, lack of transportation, lack of time, or competing time demands—tap into your support system for assistance. Who are the people in your support system?

- **Family and Friends:** Your family and friends will always support you and be your biggest cheerleaders. Your parents, grandparents, siblings, aunts, uncles, or cousins will support you in almost any way they can. Whether you need extra money to make rent, buy groceries, purchase a bus pass or train pass, or perhaps swap out childcare or elder care duties, they will support you. Your friends, or at least your true friends, will always have your back for anything you need, whether it's bumming a ride, getting a meal, or borrowing a few bucks.

- **Colleagues and Classmates:** Colleagues and classmates will be an invaluable resource. Many of them will be your lifelong friends. Colleagues can help cover any workload issues you may be facing if you are overwhelmed or need time off. Classmates will be your support system as you learn and support one another. Classmates won't be able to do your work for you, but they can be an invaluable resource in helping you master course content if you find yourself stuck. If you miss class due to illness or what not, they'll be the ones to share notes.

- **Professors and Advisors:** Professors and advisors are very much a part of your support system. By definition, their jobs are to teach you and support you in your academic goals. If you have problems with your classes, they are the first people you should contact. If you are having problems with class content, visit your professors during office hours for help. If you face challenges with other things, your advisors are among those you should see. If you are facing challenges in your personal life that you need accommodations for, such as course assignments or extensions, those arrangements should be made with your instructors. By and large, your instructors are reasonable people who are willing to work with you if you need accommodations. What often happens, though, is students don't make their challenges or needs known, so they don't get the accommodations they need or would have otherwise had. I've seen it on my end as an instructor, and as a student, I have been guilty of not seeking help from instructors when I should have. The adage "You don't ask, you don't get" always holds true. Be sure to speak up if you need something. We'll be visiting this concept again over the next few chapters.

- **Tutors:** Your tutors are among your support network with regard to academics and class subjects. If you're having trouble mastering course content, tutors are invaluable resources.

- **Outside Support Professionals:** Colleges employ a multitude of support professionals and paraprofessionals to help you succeed. Whether you need subject matter experts, like tutors or counselors; simply a friendly ear for you to vent to, like peer mentors or counselors; or housing assistance or childcare assistance, there are people on campus who can help you acquire the services you need or point you in the right direction.

Your support network in college, as in life, will help you cope with and work through any life stressors that arise.

Adjust Your Thinking

"Thinking positive" may sound cliché, but keeping a positive attitude definitely helps the stress management process. Remember that you are always in control of and responsible for your reactions and attitude.

Some of the stressful situations you may face may be dire. It is not easy being suddenly evicted and needing to find a place to live. Facing domestic violence and fearing for your safety and life is very harrowing. Having your car break down or be totaled in a car accident and, thus, losing your primary method of transportation is very stressful. All three of these situations are major stressors and major obstacles to overcome. However, you still have control over your reactions. You can choose to freak out and fill yourself with dread and worry, or you can keep your wits about you and do your best to think of solutions to get yourself into a better position.

Maintaining a positive "can do" attitude is important. Surrendering to fear and debilitating yourself with needless stress and worry will not do you as much good as staying collected and taking proactive steps for improving your situation.

Learning to *reframe negative thoughts to positive ones* is also an invaluable tool that will get you through tough times. It is cliché to say, "Look at the bright side of things," but doing so will help you stay in better spirits and keep your wits about you rather than focusing on and despairing over the negative.

Reading, listening, and watching positive media will also help you stay in a positive frame of mind. Listen to positive and uplifting music on your iPod, Pandora, or Spotify. Watch fun or uplifting and inspirational shows or movies on TV or the web. Subscribe to inspirational or uplifting Facebook pages that post positive sayings.

Finally, take some time to *learn and read Scripture* from whatever faith you believe in. The power of Scripture has sustained generations of people for millennia. The power of prayer and faith is empowering. I'll cover this topic in more depth in Chapter 32.

Keep Things in Perspective

Another tip in dealing with stressors is to keep things in perspective rather than blow things out of proportion and overreact. Students who place too much weight on grades are typically culprits of this error. Is getting an A- instead of an A that big a deal? Is getting a C on a test or even an F the end of the world? Some questions to ask yourself in such situations are:

- Does this matter in the big picture?
- Will this matter in a year? In three months? In two weeks?

More often than not, the answer is no. Things usually aren't insurmountable, and when they are, resign yourself to whatever consequences there may be. If you don't pass a class, you don't pass a class. You'll just need to retake it; that may suck, but it's not the end of the world.

Manage Your Expectations

You can better manage your stress by maintaining realistic expectations. Sometimes, our mental and emotional stresses are caused by our having unrealistic expectations. Was it realistic to write a thirty-page research paper in a single evening vs. writing it every night for five nights? Maintaining realistic expectations about situations can help you avoid disappointments and anguish.

Get Enough Exercise

One of the biggest stress management techniques overall is to get regular exercise—ideally daily. Your regular exercise regimen should include a combination of cardio, resistance training, and stretching exercises.

High intensity activities are great for burning calories, expending excess energy, and working off stress and anxieties. Some popular workouts nowadays include:

- Running
- Kickboxing
- Jiu-jitsu

- Spinning
- Crossfit
- Insanity
- Bootcamp classes

In addition to high intensity activities, you may find inner peace and improved health through some mind-body activities. Examples of popular mind-body activities include:

- Yoga
- Tai Chi
- Martial Arts
- Breathing Exercises
- Chi Kung
- Meditation

Any type of exercise is a valid activity to help you control your stress and improve your health. Whether it's aerobics, dance classes, dancing at a club, a pick-up basketball game, skateboarding, swimming, kayaking, or canoeing, any physical activity is good for your body and, ultimately, your mind.

Find Relaxing Activities

In addition to regular exercise, take some time to engage in relaxation activities. Here are some additional relaxation activities you can consider incorporating regularly:

> **Massage:** Relaxing, loving, and positive touch can do a lot to improve your stress levels. Getting professional massages may be costly or cost-prohibitive, especially on a student budget, but

you can always ask a significant other, trusted friend, or family member to massage your shoulders or back once or twice a week. You'll notice it can make all the difference in your mood or stress level.

Hiking: Hiking can be a fairly strenuous form of exercise depending on the trails you hike. I list hiking under relaxing activities due to its connection to nature. For many, getting back out in nature can be a very relaxing activity in and of itself.

Going to the Beach: Going to the beach or a lake, river, or stream (as with hiking) can be therapeutic because it allows you to connect back to nature. Water also has many curative and therapeutic properties, and being near or immersed in water can do much to heal your stress.

Visiting a Park: A simple walk in a park with its beautiful landscaping can serve nicely as your nature escape if going to the mountains or beach is travel prohibitive for your schedule.

Listening or Creating Music: As a universal language, music relaxes and allows you to express yourself. Whether you're listening to music on your mp3 player or online, or making music by singing or playing an instrument, using music as an outlet will always improve your mood and help you blow off some stress.

Spending Time with Pets: Studies show that connecting with animals helps people lower their stress levels and improve their moods and outlooks. The unconditional loving nature of animals and the symbiotic connections we form with them allow us to discharge our stresses. If you have a pet, take the time to connect with him or her. If you don't have a pet, consider volunteering or working at an animal shelter, boarding, or daycare facility.

Any of the above relaxation activities will help you manage your stress and should be part of your stress-management plan.

Get Enough Sleep

Finally, but perhaps most importantly, be sure you are getting adequate sleep. Most Americans are sleep-deprived from needing to hold down a few jobs to get by. As a student who may be working and trying to find time to study, chances are you probably are sleep-deprived. Don't take sleep for granted. Be sure you're getting enough sleep in your schedule when and where you can, even if it's on the bus or train ride home or en route to your jobs.

Preventative Mental Health Treatment

Proper stress management is important for maintaining good mental health. Just as you should brush your teeth and floss daily to maintain good dental health, managing your stress is important to maintain your mental health and prevent mental health emergencies. To review, you should:

- Manage your stressors
- Exercise regularly
- Maintain healthy relationships with family, friends, colleagues, and significant others
- Avoid drugs and manage alcohol

We've talked about managing your stress and exercising regularly in the previous sections. Staying engaged and keeping solid relationships with those in your support system like family, friends, colleagues, and classmates is also critical for maintaining your mental health. When life gets overwhelming, your family, friends, colleagues, or classmates can help you remove or alleviate some of the stressors in your life. Reach out and share your needs with the people in your support network. I'll talk more about asking for help in Chapter 29.

Finally, this should go without saying, but it is best to avoid drugs and manage your usage of alcohol. Drug and alcohol addictions will only exacerbate your stress, get you into financial and legal troubles, and ruin your relationships with your loved ones. Many students view their college experience as a time to spread their wings, sow their wild oats, and experiment with alcohol and drugs. You're an adult and responsible for your own decisions. Smart people avoid drugs and avoid or limit their alcohol for their own good.

Mental Health Treatment

Sometimes, managing your stress is not enough. Sometimes, life can become overwhelming and basic coping mechanisms like exercise or positive thinking may just not be enough. In such times, you may want or need to seek out treatment from a mental health professional like a psychiatrist or therapist.

Many Americans suffer from psychiatric conditions like anxiety or depression. If you find yourself experiencing these issues or other psychiatric conditions, know that it is perfectly common and normal to suffer from them, just as if you had other health problems with heart disease, hypertension, diabetes, or cancer. There is no shame in it.

Psychiatrists are medical doctors who can prescribe medications to help you manage anxiety, depression, or other mental health disorders. Therapists can provide you with perspective on the issues you are facing.

If you have developed issues with alcohol or drug abuse, mental health professionals can help you treat your dependency issues.

Finally, there are support groups and intensive programs where you can meet others who are going through life's problems just as you are. There's a lot of help and resources out there.

Suicide and suicide ideation is a common problem that plagues students and professionals of all ages when their coping mechanisms fail them in the midst of some of life's biggest stresses. Whatever you may be facing, know that bad times always pass, whether it's a bad grade in a course, a failing or abusive relationship, or even homelessness. If you find yourself at a point in life where everything seems overwhelming and you are considering ending it all, get help from a mental health professional immediately and tap into your support network to take care of whatever stressors are getting the better of you. Part of succeeding in college and in life is being able to weather the storms until the sunshine comes out again and you live to fight another day.

SUMMARY

In this chapter, we talked about stress management. We defined what stress is and how you can assess your stress levels. We talked about identifying your stressors and delegating, deferring, and declining commitments to unload some of the stressors facing you. We talked about the importance of knowing yourself and what your stressors are. From there, we talked about managing your thinking and your reactions to life's stressors; you may or may not have control over the situations you are forced to face in life, but you can always control how you react to them. We talked about stress management techniques, including reaching out to your support network, controlling your thinking, getting regular exercise, and engaging in relaxation activities. Finally, we talked about reaching out to mental health professionals if you find yourself unable to cope with life's stressors, despite your usage of good stress management techniques.

> "Being in control of your life and having realistic expectations about your day-to-day challenges are the keys to stress management, which is perhaps the most important ingredient to living a happy, healthy and rewarding life."
>
> — Marilu Henner

YOUR COLLEGE AND LIFE ROADMAP

Stress management is a critical life skill you will need to master throughout your life. Let's put together a solid stress management plan for you.

Exercise 1: What Are Your Stressors?

- Take some time to identify what your stressors in life are.
- What are some situations that give you stress?
- Are there certain people in your life with whom you have stressful relationships or interactions?
- Are there certain activities that give you stress? Certain places? Note what your stressors are.

Exercise 2: Time Management Revisited

Review what your current commitments are in your school, work, family, and social lives. Can you adequately handle your responsibilities? If the answer is no, what can you delegate to others? What can you defer till a later time? What do you need to decline?

Exercise 3: Your Thinking

Sometimes, you can't control the situations you are in. Sometimes, you can. But you can always control your reactions and how you think. List some stressful situations you encounter fairly regularly. Practice reframing your thinking about these situations from negative thoughts to more positive ones. In situations you cannot control, all you can do is accept them for what they are and move on.

For situations in the past, you must simply let them go and move on because the past cannot be changed.

Exercise 4: Your Support System

Part of stress management is knowing whom to turn to when things get rough. Spend some time identifying trusted family members, friends, colleagues, or college staff you can turn to if things come up.

>   Trusted Family Members:
>
>   Trusted Friends:
>
>   Trusted Co-Workers:
>
>   Trusted Classmates:
>
>   College Faculty and Staff:

Exercise 5: Exercise

What are some exercise activities or physical activities you like to engage in? Find a way to schedule them into your life to relieve your stress.

Exercise 6: What Relaxes You?

What relaxation activities do you like to engage in? Find a way to schedule time for them to relieve your stress.

Exercise 7: Mental Health Professionals

In the event you ever need the assistance of a mental professional, it'll be good to know a few in your area you can turn to. See if you can get some recommendations from your primary care physician.

    Psychiatrist:

    Psychologist/Therapist:

28

BUILDING YOUR SUPPORT NETWORK—THEY'VE GOT YOUR BACK

"Every great athlete, artist and aspiring being has a great team to help them flourish and succeed—personally and professionally. Even the so-called 'solo star' has a strong supporting cast helping them shine, thrive and take flight."

— Rasheed Ogunlaru

A Look Back, a Look Ahead

In Chapter 27, we looked at stress management. In this chapter, I will expand on one of the key concepts to stress management as well as college and life success in general—building a strong support network.

What Does a Support Network Have to Do with Life?

Life is not something done in isolation. We require the help and support of others to accomplish things. There is no such things as a "self-made" person. Wherever it is you go in life and whatever it is you do, you'll need to learn how to cultivate and build support networks, whether you're trying to get through college, build a career, or organize a movement to improve your community. If you've been an athlete on a team or served in the armed forces, you know the value of teamwork. In this chapter, I'll discuss how to build up your support team to see you through your college years so you can not only survive but thrive.

Your Support Network

Throughout this book, we've talked about the importance of forming positive relationships and connections with people. In Chapter 6, we discussed learning about campus resources and providers. In Chapters 8 and 23, we talked about building relationships with your classmates. In Chapter 22, we talked about building relationships with your instructors. In the last chapter, we talked about having a support network to help you alleviate some of the stressors in your life. In this chapter, we will put it all together to talk about your overall support network both within school and your life. College is just one facet of your life, but your college success is impacted by things going on in your life outside of college. Your college support network will need to include people from outside of school as well. One does not happen in isolation of the other.

Campus Support Network

To review from Chapter 6, you'll want to build a good campus support network. Knowing the services on campus and who the providers are by name and person is important. Your campus support network should include:

- Instructor(s)
- Your academic counselor(s)/advisor(s)
- Program coordinators and staff for support services you qualify for
- Financial aid staff
- Librarians
- Tutors
- Peer mentors
- Your classmates
- Your residence hall advisor and other housing staff (if you live on campus)
- Your roommates/dorm mates
- Your coaches and athletics staff (if an athlete)

It's important always to remember that college staff are employed to assist you in your learning. Many of the support staff are employed to help you connect with on- or off-campus resources if outside school factors start to impact your ability to learn. If you come across funding, transportation, childcare, medical, housing, or other issues, typically a staff member can assist you. Your advisor is usually a good first point of contact for such issues.

If you're having issues with specific classes, your support network should include your instructor, your classmates, and support staff in the learning assistance or tutoring centers and library.

Off-Campus Support

Just as critical as your on-campus support network is your off-campus support network. These folks can typically help you with things outside the classroom that may impact your performance in school. Life happens to everyone. Be sure you know whom you can turn to when things go wrong in your life. Your off-campus support network may include:

- Family
- Significant Other
- Friends
- Pastor/reverend/rabbi or other religious leader
- Boss/coworkers/colleagues

Support Needed

Here's a list of things you'll want to call on your support team for help with and whom to ask for help:

- **Homework, assignments, research:** People you can turn to include your classmates, instructors, tutors, librarians, and other campus learning assistance support staff.

- **Change in work schedule:** Go to your boss or perhaps your coworkers who can change shifts or hours with you.

- **Workload reduction:** Your boss or coworkers willing to take more hours or take over projects from you.

- **Meals:** Family, friends, significant others, or roommates, who can either help prepare meals if you're short on cooking time or who can spot you meals if you're low on money.

- **Money:** Bank of Mom and Dad will almost always be willing to help you if they can. You can ask trusted friends to spot you if needed. Employers may also be willing to do advances on pay if they have programs like that available. Or you can always try to find a better paying job or take on extra work on the side.

- **Chores and family responsibilities:** Other family members or trusted friends who can help you cover for any errands or chores you need to do if you need to free up time to study or get work done in a time crunch.

- **Childcare:** Family members or trusted friends who can watch your kids. If need be, you can always hire a babysitter based on references or referrals from others.

- **Rides:** Family, friends, or roommates can always hook you up with a ride. Services like Uber or Lyft can also get you where you need to go. Many colleges offer ride share connection services for people traveling to and from the same areas.

- **Venting:** At times, we all just need to vent! If you're venting about school, great ears include your classmates, roommates, tutors, peer mentors, or a trusted counselor on campus. Friends or family members work too.

- **Talking through a problem:** Sometimes, you need an ear to listen or you need good feedback to work through a problem. Friends and family can always do this. Counselors on campus can also assist. If you need a professional therapist, you may consider finding a good one in your area.

- **Massages:** Never underestimate the power of a nice

relaxing massage. You can always hire a massage therapist if you have the money, or sometimes a trusted friend works just fine.

- **Activity partners:** You can't always be studying. Sometimes, you just need to go out and have some fun. Friends, roommates, or classmates make great activity partners for whatever you choose to do, whether you're hitting up a club, catching a movie, going for a workout, or vegging out by playing video games or watching the tube or a movie.

SUMMARY

In this chapter, we talked about building a good support network at and outside of school for any challenges that could affect your school performance. I provided a short list of situations that can come up and folks you can turn to. Know who your campus support providers are. Build a strong support system at home and outside of school with your friends. Your employers and coworkers are also a part of your support system. If you need professional support and help, know which providers in your area you can turn to.

> "Surround yourself with people who provide you with support and love and remember to give back as much as you can in return."
>
> — Karen Kain

YOUR COLLEGE AND LIFE ROADMAP

Supportive people in your life will help you through the challenges you face. Let's take some time to identify and name some of them.

Name all of your instructors.

Name a friend or two in each class.

Name your academic counselor/advisor.

Name the support program coordinators you are eligible to use.

Who are your roommates?

Who are the residence hall staff or your building's resident manager or landlord?

If you need something fixed at home, whom can you ask?

If you're running late for class and need a ride, whom can you call?

If you need a ride late at night, whom can you call?

If you are short on money to pay your bills, whom can you call?

If you need a good ear to listen to you, whom can you call?

If you need to blow off some steam and go do something, whom are you going to call?

29

ASKING FOR HELP IS OKAY—IT'S THE SMART THING TO DO

"The purpose of human life is to serve and to show compassion and the will to help others."

— Albert Schweitzer

A Look Back, a Look Ahead

In Chapter 28, we revisited and expanded on the importance of building your support network to help you succeed in your studies as well as your life. We all get by and succeed with the help and support of our loved ones, friends, and other supporters. In this chapter, we explore the importance of asking for help when you need it. Many students are held back because they take too long to ask for assistance when needed.

What Does Asking for Help Have to Do with Life?

Knowing when to ask for help is a critical life skill. Throughout life, you will always encounter challenging situations. While it is admirable to try to be self-sufficient and do things for yourself, sometimes you need to know when it is time to ask for help. There is never any shame in asking for assistance when needed.

The Myth of Independence

Western society thrives on the image of self-made people and independence from others. Being self-sufficient is an admirable goal, and for the most part, I'd like to think that most of us can exist rather independently. The truth of the matter, though, is that no one is 100 percent independent—we all are interconnected and dependent on each other for mutual survival. The food you buy in the store was grown by farmers, processed, and transported to the store. The money you earn to buy your food and pay your utilities is earned through an employer who pays you, and who, in turn, receives that money from customers and clients. The electricity that lights your home and powers your Internet or TV comes from an electric company. Even if you are living on your own and make enough money to pay your rent, you are not fully independent. You rely on the products and services of others to live the quality of life you want.

Self-Sufficiency Is Admirable

While our goal in life is to be as self-sufficient as possible, sometimes you need to know when to admit you need help with something. By definition, school is not easy. As a student, you are learning things that are new to you. Some concepts you'll catch on to very easily. Some things you may need time and help to process and understand better. Sometimes, you'll need help to understand these things. Despite your own individual best efforts, such as reviewing your notes, looking online for resources, etc., you may still need to or at least want to double-check with others to make sure your understanding is in line with everyone else's. Affirmation is always a good thing.

No Such Thing as a Dumb Question

From our time in high school, we may have bought into the myth of asking dumb questions. The reality is that there is no such thing as a dumb question. If you don't know something, you don't know it, and there's no shame in that. Ultimately, you don't want to worry about what other people think. If you need to ask a clarifying question so you can understand something better, ask your question. It's better to ask a question and have people think you're dumb than to stay silent, not learn, and remain ignorant. Another thing to consider is that often others are in the exact same position as you. They don't really know or understand something, but they are too scared to ask from fear of looking stupid. The only thing stupid is not asking a question when you don't understand something or need help because then you remain confused, uninformed, or stuck.

No Shame in Asking for Help

The key thing to remember, whether you're in class, at the learning assistance/tutoring center, talking to a librarian, or anywhere else is if you need help or have a question, ask for what you need. Remember, college faculty and staff are paid to assist you.

If you're too shy to ask a question in class, ask your instructor in private during his or her office hours, or you can also always email your instructor for assistance.

Librarians are always there to help you find books or journal articles, or aid you in your research.

Counselors are there to provide information, give advice about college policies, help you select your courses, or point you to other resources you need.

Tutors are there to assist you in learning subject matters in their area of expertise.

Help Desk students are there to help you with anything relevant they are knowledgeable about.

Staff are paid to assist you. Get your money's worth by getting the information and help you need. Always ask.

Let me tell you a story that illustrates the need to ask for help. One of my past jobs was running a tutoring program. One of the students who came into the tutoring center was sitting at a desk doing his work. At one point, he became very frustrated and complained to another staff member that no one was helping him. The other staff member asked him, "Did you ask for help?" When he said, "No," she reaffirmed that he needed to initiate asking for help. At no point had he gotten in line to see a tutor or raised his hand for other staff to assist him. He did not ask for the help he needed, and thus, he didn't receive any.

You Don't Ask…

You don't ask, you don't get. Always remember that.

Self-Advocacy

One of the key success skills for college and life you'll ultimately want to develop is being your own self-advocate. You need to be able to get out there and know how to request the information and support you need. While growing up, you may have had the luxury of your parents or an older sibling being the person to go out there and find the information, help, and services you needed. But as a young adult in college, it's your time to be independent, so take the initiative to ask for the help you need.

You'll find there are a lot of helpful people out there, but not everyone may necessarily know you need help if you don't ask, much like that student who came to do his work in the tutoring center. Never assume people know what you need. People are not mind readers. Be sure to ask specifically for what it is you need.

Accept Help When It Is Offered

Perhaps equally important to asking for help is not being too proud to accept help when it is offered to you. Many times, you will be able to do something for yourself without help and assistance from others, which is great. Sometimes, though, it may be silly and foolish to put yourself through an unnecessary experience where you are clearly in need when a nice stranger is willing to help you.

Once when preparing to leave school, I saw my car had a flat tire. I knew how to change a flat, but I will be the first to admit I am not overly good at it. Another student came upon me trying to change it. Seeing I was having some trouble, he offered to help. I could have changed my tire on my own, but it would have taken me a while. Knowing I'd be up and running quicker with this fellow student's help, I readily accepted.

In another instance, I once went on a hike up a very steep trail. I didn't pack enough water with me for the hike and had run out. I took a break up the trail to catch my breath. A few hikers were making their way down and passed me. Seeing me a bit winded and without water, they offered me one of their extra bottles. I graciously accepted their water, thanked them, and wished them well. Had I not taken their water, I'd have been perfectly fine; I was in no danger of fainting or dying on the trail, but I would've been hot, thirsty, and slightly dehydrated. I was grateful for their generous help.

One life success lesson is to be willing to accept help from others, even though you may feel you'll be okay without it. There is no shame in accepting help, especially if it will get you to your goal quicker.

SUMMARY

In this chapter, we talked about the important skill of knowing when to ask for help. Wanting to do things on your own is okay. But sometimes, the most expedient way to reach your goal is to ask for assistance, especially when you are struggling. Asking questions does not make you look stupid; it helps you to learn better. Staying silent when you are unclear is a recipe for remaining ignorant. Always ask for the help you need and be willing to accept assistance when it is offered. There is no dumb question. If you do not ask, you do not get.

> "Make me help myself, make me learn to do things I need on my own, make me not feel bad for getting help."
>
> — Jordan Hoechlin

YOUR COLLEGE AND LIFE ROADMAP

Knowing when to ask for help is a critical life skill. Equally critical is being receptive to accepting help from others. Let's practice these skills.

Exercise 1: Asking for Help

Over the next week, be mindful of the times when you need assistance and ask for the help you need. Prior to this, would you have chosen to remain silent and "figure things out on your own"? Or would you have asked for help regardless?

Exercise 2: Accepting Help

Over the next week, be mindful of the times when people offer to assist you with something. Do you accept their help, or do you decline, choosing to do things on your own? Take some opportunities to accept assistance if and when it is offered.

30

FAILING IS OKAY—YOU CAN'T WIN THEM ALL

> "Failure should be our teacher, not our undertaker. Failure is delay, not defeat. It is a temporary detour, not a dead end. Failure is something we can avoid only by saying nothing, doing nothing and being nothing."
>
> — Denis Waitley

A Look Back, a Look Ahead

In the previous chapter, we discussed knowing when to ask for help and accepting help when it is offered. In this chapter, we will discuss failure.

What Does Failure Have to Do with Life?

Failure is a part of life. While no one ever sets out to fail at things, you simply cannot win them all. Knowing to accept failure and then to get back up and try again is one of life's biggest lessons.

Part of succeeding in college and in life is recognizing failure for what it is—a learning experience. Bouncing back from failures and learning from them is what success is all about.

The Fear of Failure

One of life's biggest fears is the fear of failure. We are raised in a society that always prides itself on and rewards success. Only winners are ever recognized. Losing or failing is a stigma. It cultivates in us an aversion to failing and losing. However, the truth of the matter is that failure is a part of life, and every winner at one time failed at something or lost. It is impossible to win at everything or to be the best all the time.

The Trouble of Perfectionism

Many students, particularly high achievers, may suffer from perfectionism. The dictionary defines perfectionism as "a personality trait characterized by a person's striving for flawlessness and setting excessively high performance standards, accompanied by overly critical self-evaluations and concerns regarding others' evaluations."

As a practice, we always want to strive to do our best, but at the same time, we want to let go of the unrealistic expectation of ourselves to be perfect. As students, we are in the process of learning a skill or knowledge set. As beginners and learners, we will inevitably make mistakes and are not expected to be experts right out the door. If you drop a grade on an assignment or a test here and there, that's perfectly normal and acceptable. Even if you're getting average grades, it's acceptable. Learning is the key point. As long as you are learning and getting better, your time has been well spent.

Do Your Best

At the end of the day, all you can do is to do your best. Prepare your best for the work you need to do. Put forth your best effort in your lessons, assignments, and exams. Do the best you can. All anyone can ask of you is to do your best, and if you fall short, you can try to do better the next time.

Sometimes You May Fail

Inevitably, despite your best efforts, sometimes you fail. Or sometimes you know you didn't put in the effort so you failed. Failure is part of life. If you're a perfectionist, you'll need to come to the realization that you can't win all the time. All students must realize that failure is part of the learning process and there is no shame in it.

As a student, you are in training for a skill or profession. The classroom is the best place for you to make mistakes and "fail" because the stakes are relatively low—it's only a grade. If you were to make similar mistakes or failures in the "real world," it could cost you your job, your customers, or your company's reputation, making it more difficult for you to get more business. It is much, much better to experience your failures and learning experiences in the relatively safe environment of a school than out in the real world where time, money, and business are at greater stake.

Three times in my academic career, I completely bombed a class or had to take an Incomplete and repeat the class. On all of those occasions, life had happened to me and kept me from completing a course. By no means was I happy about failing, but I recognized in each and every case that things out of my control had happened and these were just setbacks.

The very first time I had to repeat a class was during business school. I had a lot of things going on in my personal and professional lives that impacted my schooling. When I had to take an Incomplete for the final course I needed to graduate, I was devastated! I would not be graduating that semester as I'd planned and would need to return to school in the fall. That, along with all the other stressors happening in my life, caused me to have a nervous breakdown, and I wound up needing to get professional help to deal with the failure of school and the stressors in my life. Eventually, though, I made my comeback, finished the course and the program, and received my degree. I may not have finished when and under the circumstances I wanted, but I never gave up, and I did meet my goal eventually. "Failures" are just setbacks. The only true failure happens if you completely give up.

Keep Grades in Perspective

> "Steve Jobs, Bill Gates and Mark Zuckerberg didn't finish college. Too much emphasis is placed on formal education—I told my children not to worry about their grades but to enjoy learning."
>
> — Nassim Nicholas Taleb

Students often get too caught up in grades. Make no mistake—grades are important, but they are not the end all, be all. Grades are only one measure of your success or aptitude. I've been on job interview and admissions committees where we've hired or admitted people with lower GPAs than other applicants because they had other factors that made them more attractive. They may have brought more to the table in terms of experience or goals, or they may have had personalities that fit better with the organization or program. By all means, strive to do your best and get good grades, but don't let them be the end all measuring stick.

I've seen students who came into a course not knowing anything at all, but they still earned a C, which to me means more than a student who came into the course, already knew the material, and easily earned an A. In school, learning counts. I would say the student who earned the C learned much, much more from the course than the student who got the "Easy A."

Grades are just one measure of your learning. Don't get too bent out of shape over dropping a grade here or there. Focus on doing your best and coming away learning something of use.

Fail, Learn, and Improve

Failures are learning opportunities for us. If you didn't earn the grade you were looking for, reassess what did not work for you. Did you need to spend more time studying? Could you have seen a tutor? Worked more with a study group? Visited your professor during office hours? Were you just too overburdened with other demands to devote enough time to class? Could you take less classes in the future? Could you ask for more time off from work, or ask family members to take over your share of the chores more?

Take your instructor's feedback to heart when you get back your papers and assignments. Your instructors spend many hours grading and providing feedback on your work. The intention is to help you improve. Critiques and feedback are there to help you become better; they are not attacks on you. Keep critiques and comments in perspective, and use them as opportunities to improve.

The safe learning environment of college is the best time to make mistakes and improve because the stakes are low. You don't want to repeat these mistakes out in the real world where they can be truly costly to your career or to your customers, clients, or patients, who have their money, health and wellbeing, or very lives at stake.

It's Okay to Fail

At the end of the day, realize that it is okay to fail. We are all human. You can't win them all. Despite your best efforts, sometimes you get knocked down. What's important is that you get back up and try again. Learn from your mistakes and failures, and endeavor not to repeat them. Learn what didn't work and take the time to determine what will.

SUMMARY

In this chapter, we discussed the need to accept failure as part of the learning process and what it takes to achieve success. You won't be perfect all the time, and at times, life or a subject may get the better of you so that you need to drop a grade or course. You might need to eat an F or an Incomplete on an assignment or as a course grade. All you can do is accept the situation for what it is, move on to whatever comes next, and try again. The safe learning environment of college is a place where you can learn and make mistakes as part of your training. Mistakes in the real world can be very costly. Learn what does and doesn't work for you and move on.

> "Life is a series of experiences, each one of which makes us bigger, even though sometimes it is hard to realize this. For the world was built to develop character, and we must learn that the setbacks and grieves which we endure help us in our marching onward."
>
> — Henry Ford

YOUR COLLEGE AND LIFE ROADMAP

Failures are often our best teachers. They show us what does not work. They help us to learn about our limits, and ultimately, they show us ways we can grow to be better. Let's take some time to reflect on our failures and the lessons we have learned or need to learn so we may grow from our failures and mistakes to be better.

Exercise 1: Accepting Past Failures

Think back to times in your life when you failed. What could you have done differently to avoid failure? What could you have done differently in your reactions to times you failed?

Exercise 2: Learning from Current Failures

Have you failed at something recently? What did you learn from it? How did you improve yourself based on what you learned?

31

MAINTAINING A BALANCED LIFE AS A STUDENT—A JUGGLING ACT

> "In all aspects of our lives balance is key. Doing one thing too much can cause upset, like the old saying goes, everything in moderation is the secret."
>
> — Catherine Pulsifer

A Look Back, a Look Ahead

In the last chapter, we looked at accepting and overcoming failure. In this chapter, we will start to bring together everything you've learned in Part V on fortitude. Specifically, we will discuss how to maintain a balanced life as a college student.

What Does Balance Have to Do with Life?

Success in college and life is all about balance. We all wear various hats and fulfill various roles in life. At times, certain roles dominate. Part of balanced living is maintaining a good balance between your various obligations and commitments: school, work/career, family, relationships, and your social and personal needs. In this chapter, we will review some of the techniques covered in time management and stress management to help you maintain as balanced a life as possible during your college years.

The Life Balance Wheel

When talking about living a balanced life, a good framework is the life balance wheel. In the time management chapter, we discussed the various roles and commitments we all have. Now we must expand this concept to view ourselves in terms of additional facets of self-responsibility we need to adhere to. The life balance wheel is a great tool for self-assessing yourself to ensure all parts of your life are functioning and healthy and remain so. Here are the eight sectors of the life balance wheel to measure your life by:

1. **Finances:** This sector refers to your financial health and managing your money. Do you keep your spending under control? Are you bringing in enough money to meet your financial obligations? Are you building a nest egg to finance big purchases or for your retirement?

2. **Work and Career:** This sector refers to entering into and thriving in your chosen career or maintaining your current job to ensure you can make a living for yourself.

3. **Academics and Education:** This sector refers to your success in school and as a lifelong learner. Do you have the skills you need to progress successfully in your studies and achieve your learning goals?

4. **Health:** This sector refers to all aspects of your health. Do you maintain a proper diet and weight? Is your body physically fit in terms of cardio capacity, strength, and flexibility? Medically, how is your health? Are you treating any chronic conditions you may suffer from, or are you taking the right preventative measures to stay healthy? How is your mental health? Do you manage your stress properly?

5. **Family:** This sector refers to your familial relationships and commitments. Are you meeting your commitments and obligations as a member of your family? How are your relationships with your parents, elders, siblings, spouse, or children?

6. **Romantic Relationships:** This sector refers to your relationship with your significant other or your quest to find a significant other.

7. **Social Life:** This sector refers to your relationships with your friends and having a life outside of school or work.

8. **Spiritual:** This sector refers to your relationship with your spiritual self or Higher Power. We will explore this sector in more depth in Chapter 32.

When taken as a whole, the life balance wheel is a good tool for assessing how your life is in each of these areas. It gives you a chance to set goals to improve your life in the areas where you are lacking.

Utilize Good Time-Management Skills

Part of living a balanced life is the allocation of proper time to each part of your life to ensure you are dedicating the time needed to meet your goals. As a college student, your studies will take up a huge chunk of your time, which means you will have less time to allocate to other parts of your life. You may not have as much time for your family or friends. You may need to work less hours. You may need to forgo some of your previous workout or hobby time.

Maintaining a balanced life doesn't necessarily mean you need to eliminate those other areas from your life. In fact, balancing your life means simply taking time from certain parts of your life and allocating it to the areas where it is most needed. Do not eliminate your workout time from your life in total. Instead of working out for two hours, five days a week, you may need to cut back to two hours, three days a week. You may need to limit your social hangout time with your friends to strictly Saturday nights, instead of Friday and Saturday nights.

To ensure other parts of your life besides school are properly attended to, schedule time into your calendar for the following:

- paying bills and balancing your checkbook
- grocery shopping and preparing meals
- laundry and house cleaning
- a daily or regular workout
- taking any needed medications and regular doctors' appointments
- time with family and friends

As we learned in time management, you can free up time in your schedule by knowing when to delegate and defer tasks. Besides freeing up your time, it will help prevent work overload and burnout. You can also leverage time to multitask (doing homework or reading while commuting on the bus or while doing cardio work on a treadmill).

Schedule "Me" Time

Since most of your time will be spent attending classes, doing homework, and going to any jobs you take on to pay bills, it is important that you schedule regular "me" time so you can relax and unwind. To ensure your schedule and life is balanced, make time for the following:

- **Regular exercise:** If you're the gym type, by all means get a gym membership. If you're not the gym type, there are lots of ways to get regular exercise outside of the gym. Buy some workout videos you can do in your home. Go for a run around the block or at the park. Go swimming at the campus pool or a neighborhood pool. Play some sports games with friends such as basketball, soccer, touch football, or Frisbee. Do some yoga or tai chi in the park. Go dancing with some friends at the club or sign up for dance lessons. Join a local martial arts club or school. Even a simple walk around the neighborhood will suffice. Take time to give your body the exercise it needs. You'll feel better and look better.

- **Learn and maintain proper nutrition:** Eating properly is vital for your wellbeing. As students, money may be tight if you are living on your own without a campus meal plan. College can be a time when you fall into bad eating habits. Let's face it; when money is tight, you'll quickly learn that bad food is also the cheapest. It may save you cash, but the costs of bad nutrition will catch up with you later in life as you develop medical conditions that require medications, doctors' visits, and hospitalization. Take the time to learn about and adhere to good nutrition. More fruits and vegetables. Less chips, sodas, beers, pizzas, or instant ramen. If you must purchase meals from fast food restaurants, order the healthier meals (chicken vs. hamburger and salads vs.

fries). Avoid the value meals and sodas, and stick to either bottled water or flavor your water with things like lemon or Crystal Light.

- **Leisure and social activities:** Social activities help you to form and maintain needed bonds with family and friends and allow you to decompress from life's responsibilities in a fun way. Rent some movies if you can't afford the theatre. Attend plays at the campus or local theatre. Play video games. Hit the clubs with your friends. Go to a concert, sing karaoke, or pick up an instrument and jam a song. Social activities are some of the best ways to spend your time and make cherished memories with loved ones. When we are busy, we often neglect our loved ones. This is a costly mistake. A common regret people have on their deathbeds is that they didn't spend as much time with their loved ones because they were always working. No one on his deathbed ever wished he had spent more time working.

- **Learn about finances:** We all need money to survive in this world. Take time to learn about investing, savings strategies, and cost-saving tips. Take some time to learn about running a small business. Learning about finances is *always* time well-spent.

- **Some type of spiritual activity:** We will cover this in more depth in Chapter 32.

Take Care of Basic Needs

Another aspect of living a balanced life is simply taking care of your basic needs. As students, we can get so stressed with our studies that we may neglect our basic needs. Be sure to eat regular meals, get adequate sleep, and take care of basic grooming and hygiene needs.

SUMMARY

In this chapter, we explored living a balanced life. I introduced you to the Life Balance Wheel as a framework to ensure you are spending adequate time on the important aspects of your life. I gave you suggestions for scheduling time into your weekly and daily calendar to ensure you don't neglect important parts of your life due to the massive time commitment your studies require. To review, be sure to spend time each week on the following:

- Getting adequate sleep
- Eating regular healthy meals
- Practicing good time management
- Exercising
- Scheduling social time with loved ones and friends
- Scheduling time to take care of your finances, chores, and housekeeping needs

> "Our lives are a mixture of different roles. Most of us are doing the best we can to find whatever the right balance is…. For me, that balance is family, work, and service."
>
> — Hillary Rodham Clinton

YOUR COLLEGE AND LIFE ROADMAP

It's challenging to maintain a balanced life when most of your "free" time outside of class and work is spent doing homework. Let's adhere to the life balance wheel and explicitly schedule some "me" time.

Exercise 1: Regular Exercise

Commit some specific times in your schedule as your daily or weekly exercise times. Whatever it is you may be trying to do or accomplish, when this time in your schedule hits, drop what you are doing and commit to exercising. If you don't have time to get to the gym, do your exercises at home or take a quick walk around the block.

Exercise 2: Nutrition and Meals

Set regular daily meal times. Set up regular grocery shopping days in your week. Be sure to purchase more nutritious foods that you can stretch if you are on a strict monetary budget so you can avoid junk food.

Exercise 3: Social Time with Family and Friends

Schedule specific times to do activities with family and friends. List some activities you enjoy with the people in your life. Block out time for them on your calendar.

Exercise 4: Financial Goals

Set some financial goals for yourself. What are some finance-related things you'd like to learn more about? Take some time to research them online, via books, or by meeting with a good financial advisor.

32

NURTURING YOUR FAITH AND SPIRIT—CONNECTING WITH SOURCE

"With man this is impossible,
but with God all things are possible."

— Jesus Christ
(Matthew 19:26; Mark 10:27; Luke 18:27)

"I can do all things through Christ who strengthens me."

— Philippians 4:13

A Look Back, a Look Ahead

In Chapter 31, we discussed how you can lead a balanced life, even with the demands of being a student. In this chapter, we will take a look at how you can nurture your faith and your spirit during your college years.

What Does Faith Have to Do with Life?

Success in life includes the realization that success is powered by a connection to Source or a Higher Power. Our triumphs are owed equally to blessings from Source as to our own hard work. During the times when we struggle with challenges, cultivating and drawing strength from our faith will help us through the hard times. Developing and nurturing your relationship with your faith is important to your college and life success.

Faith and Spirit

First and foremost, faith and spirit do not necessarily refer to religion. For many people, they will be rooted in their religious beliefs, but for the purposes of this book, they refer to a belief in something greater than yourself. Through the ages, all human cultures have recognized that we exist with or because of something greater and higher than ourselves. This Higher Power has been labeled by many terms or names through the ages, including:

- God
- The gods
- Nature ("The Great Spirit")
- Ancestral Connection
- Divine Source
- Universal Connection
- Higher Self
- The Force

This chapter's purpose is not to convert you from one faith to another but to honor any religious or spiritual beliefs you may have. Ultimately, I hope to encourage you to cultivate your beliefs and connection to whatever power you believe in. Doing so will aid you in channeling that faith so it helps you achieve success in college and your other endeavors while overcoming whatever challenges come across your path.

Ways to Nurture Faith

As part of maintaining life balance, here are some ways you can nurture your faith and spirit:

- **Church service:** You may have grown up with the church as part of your life. As a college student, you may choose to continue to attend regular church services. You may elect to remain with the church you grew up with or you may choose to find a new church. If you didn't grow up with a church, this may be a time to explore and find a church that's in line with your values. There is no shortage of faiths, and your time in college may expose you to various ones. Whether you attend a Christian church, Jewish synagogue, Islamic mosque, Buddhist temple, or participate in whatever faith you come across, use the time to explore, learn, and connect with God, your Higher Power, or Divine Source.

- **College ministry:** Many colleges have campus ministries from various affiliated churches that you can participate in. Some of them are offered as campus clubs. If you are new to nurturing your faith, these may be good places to begin and find support.

- **Prayer:** If you lack the time or interest to attend regular services, religious fellowship, or studies, you can always use regular prayer as a means for nurturing your faith and spirit. Prayer is a form of invocation and of giving thanks and gratitude to whatever Higher Power you believe in. Prayers can be offered at any time and occasion, whether at the start or end of each day, before or after class, before exams, or before meals. Practicing your faith in solo, in lieu of the formal experience of a service or with others is a completely valid form of nurturing your faith and spirit.

- **Meditation:** For many who do not subscribe to a formal religion and believe in more of a personal relationship with a Divine Source or Higher Power, meditation is a way to cultivate your faith and spirit. Take time each day to meditate in order to calm the mind and center yourself before undertaking the day's tasks. In many spiritual traditions, always returning to center is a key to harnessing the energies of a Higher Power to face your challenges.

- **Mind-Body Work (Yoga, Tai Chi, martial arts):** For many folks, undertaking the practice of mind-body work such as yoga, tai chi, or some type of martial art is a way for them to nurture faith and spirit. At the heart of many of these activities, rooted in Eastern philosophy, is a connection to universal energies and power such as chi, ki, or prana, which give us our strength. The physical exercises open us up to absorbing and channeling these energies through our bodies, healing our bodies, and focusing the energies to help us face our challenges. In addition to the physical exercise that strengthens our bodies, the mental and spiritual exercise helps us focus and calm our minds and strengthen our spirits. Personally, I have always used martial arts, tai chi, and yoga training as my preferred way to nurture my personal faith and spirit. No shortage of gyms or schools exist that you can join to learn these things. Your campus may also have student clubs you can join to learn or practice.

- **Time in nature:** Many people find their connection to

a Higher Power by experiencing the beauty of creation in nature. Being in nature allows them to refresh and obtain spiritual guidance and renewal by becoming one with something greater. For many, hiking and rock climbing can be a deeply spiritual experience. Others find spiritual solace in water surfing, paddling/kayaking, and boating. Take some time to experience the beauty and power of nature and see whether it allows you to connect back to your Higher Power. Explore a forest on a nature hike. Conquer a mountain and feel on top of the world and one with the Heavens. Surrender and go with the flow of nature by being one with the surf or by sailing or paddling at sea, across a lake, or down a river. Explore the world beneath the sea by snorkeling or diving. Appreciating the beauty of the world as created by a Higher Power is one way to nurture your faith and spirit and recognize that there is, indeed, something greater than ourselves that keeps the world turning, while also reminding us of our place in the world. Your campus may offer clubs that partake in these activities. You're also welcome to join local Meet-Up groups or clubs, or just go with friends who also enjoy doing these activities.

SUMMARY

In this chapter, we discussed how to nurture our faith and spirit to help us succeed in our studies and any other challenges we face. Our connection to Source or a Higher Power feeds into and drives our success, coupled with the hard work and effort we put into our endeavors. Faith is our belief in something greater than ourselves. There are many ways to nurture our faith and spirit, including attending religious services or practicing spiritual activities like prayer and meditation. Training in mind and body activities like yoga, tai chi, or martial arts also allow us to nurture our faith and spirit while strengthening our mind and body. Finally, experiencing nature and becoming one with all its glory is another way to nurture your faith and spirit.

> "May the Force be with you."
>
> — *Star Wars*

Your College and Life Roadmap

Nurturing your faith and spirit is an important life success activity and skill. Let's take some time to find ways you can nurture your faith and spirit.

Exercise 1: Services

If you have attended services regularly or have always been interested in attending services, take some time to identify a local church or ministry you can join and attend services at.

Exercise 2: Mind-Body Activities

Mind-body activities are a great way not only to nurture your body and spirit but also to strengthen your body and focus your mind. They can become the regular exercise you participate in as part of your stress management and life balance plan. If you've never done a mind-body practice before, now may be a good time to start learning. Research some local clubs or schools you can join, whether for yoga, tai chi, karate, kung fu, judo, aikido, or tae kwon do. List below some activities you'd be interested in trying and some potential schools, clubs, or classes you can join and attend.

Exercise 3: Get Out in Nature

Whether you're hiking through the woods, climbing a mountain, or playing on the water, getting out into nature can help you nurture your faith and spirit and enhance your connection to a Higher Power. Write down some ways you can get out in nature more!

PART VI
FROM COLLEGE TO CAREER

33

DEVELOPING YOUR PRACTICAL CAREER SKILLS WHILE A STUDENT

"Every experience in your life is being orchestrated to teach you something you need to know to move forward."

— Brian Tracy

A Look Back, a Look Ahead

Throughout this book, we have talked about how the college system works, the resources available to you to succeed, the relationships you need to build to boost your success, and the success skills you need to develop. In this chapter, we will tie all of these things together to discuss what is probably most important and practical to your future life success: how to develop your career skills while still a student in school.

What Do Career Skills Have to Do with Life?

One of the basic truths you will find as you progress through school, your career, and life is that the most basic career skills you need for success are also the basic life skills you need. Success skills are transferable between all parts of your life, whether they be effective communication, managing your time and responsibilities, following through, treating people with respect, maintaining a good attitude, or any others. Successful career skills are successful life skills. Developing good job skills and habits now will carry you through your career and the rest of your life.

Hard Skills vs. Soft Skills

An important distinction to make upfront is the difference between *hard skills* and *soft skills*. College teaches you *hard skills*—the skills you need to perform within your future profession. Examples of hard skills include:

- accounting skills and number crunching for accountants
- medical diagnosis and treatments for doctors
- engineering skills for engineers

Soft skills are those things you are not formally taught in school that are just as, if not more, important than hard skills, such as your work habits, people skills, and professionalism qualities. Many employers lament the lack of soft skills new graduates often have when they enter the workforce.

Soft Skills Examples

Following are examples of soft skills you will want to hone during your time in college.

Punctuality

Punctuality means being on time for your commitments. You need to arrive on time for your job. You need to arrive on time for appointments you make with people. You need to finish assignments on time. Being late for work, appointments, or assignments can cause distress for your colleagues, clients, and people in general. If you arrive late for work, your colleague who is working the shift before you may not be able to clock out because coverage is required. Other colleagues may need to cover for you. If you are late for appointments, it is disrespectful of the time of the person waiting for you. Finally, if you are late with completing assignments, it may have adverse effects on clients. Imagine if you are a baker tasked with making a wedding cake or if you are a fashion designer commissioned to make a custom wedding gown and you are late. It would have a disastrous effect on the bride and her wedding. If you are a payroll clerk who is late in processing people's paychecks, it will adversely impact the employees' ability to pay their own bills on time. Punctuality is very important. If you anticipate being late for work, or you cannot make an appointment or complete an assignment on time, give the people effected as much notice as possible so they can plan accordingly. Being on time is a skill you learn indirectly in college simply by arriving to class on time, turning in your assignments on time, and keeping appointments with your professors, counselors, and classmates.

Teamwork

The ability to work with others is a core skill you will need to develop. You will always need to work with others, be it your coworkers, employees, a partner, clients, or vendors. Teamwork means being able to do your part of the task at hand, whether you need to work as part of a team within your department, across departments, or across organizations. If you own your own company, you will need to work as a team with your employees or partners to accomplish your mission. Three core skills people often lack when working in a team environment are:

1. Poor communication skills
2. Lack of professionalism, i.e., being difficult to work with
3. Not doing their part, i.e., free riding.

Most underperforming teams suffer from some form of poor communication, with the right hand not communicating with the left, which can cause either redundant work efforts, tasks falling through the cracks, misunderstandings, or hard feelings. Lack of professionalism takes many forms, but it most often stems from inappropriate communication, lack of emotional intelligence, or just outright deliberate nastiness on people's parts. People not doing their part stems from them not knowing their part, lack of skills or training to complete the work, or utter laziness. While in college, you will have ample opportunity to practice both formal and informal teamwork, either through group assignments or the informal study groups you form with your peers. Practice and be mindful of developing good teamwork skills: communicate your needs with your team, do your part to the best of your ability, and treat your classmates professionally. If you can develop these habits now, you will be a rock star performer in your workplace and earn the respect of your peers.

Customer Service and Client Interaction

Employers often report that while new college graduates can perform the technical skills of their profession, they fail at the people skills component of interacting with customers and clients. The failings often come in not meeting the customer's need, not resolving their issue, or unprofessional communication and service. The two key things to learn while in school are:

1. Meet the needs of the person you are doing something for.

2. Treat and communicate with people in a professional manner.

As you go through your college experience, think of the people you interact with as your customers or clients, which may include your instructors who give you an assignment or team members on any form of a group project. As in the real business world, you are providing a product or service to specification for a customer or client, whether you are treating an illness, delivering an architectural design, developing a software program, or fixing someone's computer. Since your professor is your customer, always strive to meet his or her need by meeting the requirements in your assignments to the best of your ability. Secondly, treat him as a professional by being respectful in your dealings with him. If you're working with your classmates on group projects or in informal study groups, consider them your customers or clients as well. Always fulfill any commitments you have made to them and do the part you agreed to. Communicate with respect to your classmates.

Phone and Email Etiquette and Communication Skills

Phone and email etiquette skills are another area where employers often find that college graduates are sorely lacking. When answering the phone, state the name of your organization and your name. For example, "Thank you for calling XYZ Company. This is Judy." Be sure to listen to the caller and confirm his needs or request. Then pass the caller on to whoever can best resolve his problem or take a message and make sure the appropriate person follows up with the customer. In terms of email etiquette, be sure to write in complete sentences and maintain a professional tone. While in college, you can practice this in your emails to professors, counselors, college staff, and classmates. A common problem is "flame emails" where arguments break out. One very common situation that pops up is the "tone" of a message. Written communication, be it an email, or even a comment on an Internet message board or a Facebook post often does not convey tone properly. What may seem to be a harmless joke to you or an innocent comment may come across as very offensive or disrespectful to the person reading your message. In terms of phone etiquette, leave professional voice messages on the phones of professors and college staff, clearly stating your name, needs, and contact information. Often, professors and staff will receive calls without a clear name or phone number so they can't return a call, or they will receive harsh messages; no matter the situation, be professional in your tone and words.

Time Management

Often, employers will comment that graduates have trouble juggling multiple work tasks and are unable to budget their time appropriately to meet deadlines. Tasks not completed on time can adversely affect budgets and production schedules or delay processing times for administrative tasks like supply orders or payments. Some of the skills we've covered, such as negotiated deferment of tasks, delegation of tasks, or saying no to tasks and communicating your needs are skills that can help manage tasks. Time management is a skill you should master in school as you juggle your study time, homework time, family commitments, job commitments, and personal time.

Following Up or Following Through

Following up or following through means completing assignments to full completion as outlined and required and also making sure people you are waiting on stay on the timeline you need. This is difficult to manage given workloads and other tasks we take on or are asked to take on, but it is critical because otherwise things can "fall through the cracks," which can later come back to bite you or your organization. Following up or following through is an important soft skill you need to develop. If you work in sales, your company's lifeblood is tied to following up with sales leads and following through to close deals and ensure that customers and clients' needs are met. You will practice following up and following through during your college career by completing your course assignments and the tasks you commit to with your fellow classmates for group projects or informal study groups.

Use College as Your Time to Develop Your Soft Skills and Habits

If you are mindful of the soft skills discussed above and apply them as a college student, you should, by the time you graduate, have a solid soft skill set. You'll be a professional communicator, team player, have solid time management abilities, and be prompt in your work and attendance. You'll be a coveted worker in any organization and have the respect of your employers and peers.

College Is an Extended Job Interview

One key to success is to treat your college experience as an extended job interview. In order to succeed in the workplace, you need a good combination of *hard skills* and *soft skills*. College, by design, will give you the hard skills you need to enter your profession. It can also give you the soft skills you need, but you need to be aware of what they are and how the college experience can help you build them. Ultimately, you will want to build your hard and soft skills simultaneously.

If you remember that college is an extended job interview, then consider your professors, particularly those in your major, as your bosses who are interviewing and evaluating you. At the end of your degree program, your professors, while they may not specifically hire you for a job, will write you letters of recommendation for jobs or provide you with job leads. Your professors are respected professionals in their fields, so many employers often solicit professors for promising graduates, or they forward recruiting notices to them to forward to graduates. As such, your professors and counselors are some of your best leads for jobs (or further schooling) after you graduate. Your goal as a student and upon graduation is to earn a good recommendation and job lead from your professors.

During your college years, and especially during your major work, show your professors that you can perform the tasks of your profession with competence—prove that you have the hard skills to do the job. Through your interaction with them and your classmates and during internship or practicum experiences, show that you also have the soft skills to excel in the job world. Arrive to class on time. Finish assignments on time. If you are not able to complete tasks or arrive on time, provide advance notice and make arrangements. Communicate with them professionally on the phone or via email. If professors have made accommodations for you, then do your part to complete your assignments as agreed. Keep any appointments you've made with them. If assigned group work, ensure that they know you've done your part of the work. Come across as a professional. If you can do all of that, you'll have earned a solid recommendation from your professors for any job in your field or advanced training for your field at other institutions.

SUMMARY

Soft skills are also life success skills that will make you a rock star in your field, earning you the respect of your peers, and carry you throughout your life. Soft skills are also what employers feel graduating students need the most help with. Be mindful of soft skills that employers look for and use your time in college to hone them. Treat college as an extended job interview. Develop the hard skills of your profession while also developing your soft skills during your time in college. Think of your professors as your bosses, who are evaluating your job performance. As a reward for doing good work, they will write solid recommendation letters and provide you with job leads as you prepare to graduate.

> "What is the recipe for successful achievement? To my mind there are just four essential ingredients: Choose a career you love, give it the best there is in you, seize your opportunities, and be a member of the team."
>
> — Benjamin F. Fairless

YOUR COLLEGE AND LIFE ROADMAP

Which soft skills do you feel you need to improve on the most?

34

FINDING A POST-COLLEGE JOB WHILE A STUDENT— MAKING YOUR NEXT MOVE

"One important key to success is self-confidence. An important key to self-confidence is preparation."

— Arthur Ashe

A Look Back, a Look Ahead

In the previous chapter, we discussed what soft skills are, their role in your career and life, and how you can develop them while in college. We also discussed how you can frame college as an extended job interview and how your goal is to earn your professors' recommendations by showing you've developed both the hard skills of your profession and the soft skills required for career success. In this chapter, we will continue to discuss your post-college career by exploring how you can find a post-college job in your career field while still a student.

What Does Finding a Post-College Job Have to Do with Life?

The time between graduation and the start of your career marks a transition point in your life from one phase to the next. You will have similar phases throughout your life as you climb the career ladder or transition to different careers or life phases. The key thing is to remember that you should always have a transition or contingency plan in place to make calculated moves in the event that life happens to you and you *must* make a transition by necessity.

Finding a Post-College Job

In the following sections, we will go over strategies and techniques to help you effectively lay the groundwork to land a post-college job while still a student. While I cannot guarantee any of these will work because many factors go into getting a job, including the supply and demand of jobs and candidates in your field, many of these techniques will help you get your foot in the door and build your professional resume and network so that, over time, you can develop and land an ideal position for yourself.

Impress Your Professors

In the last chapter, we talked about treating college as an extended job interview and how your professors are your employers. As mentioned, professors are respected professionals in their and your field, so they are often looked to by employers to identify good candidates for positions. You will want to leverage their relationships and connections to find job leads or earn solid recommendation letters from them for jobs in your field. Throughout your degree program, build the hard skills your professors are teaching you while also developing your soft skills to show that you are a quality professional ready to enter the field. If you can do so, you will earn a solid recommendation letter that you can, hopefully, use to leverage the network your professors have and strengthen your job prospects.

Internship/Practicum

To help you develop practical job skills before you enter your profession, many programs require an internship or practicum experience or they offer it as an elective. If it is required in your program, do your best to succeed as an intern. If it is an elective, take advantage of the opportunity. An internship or practicum allows you to get on-the-job experience in an organization and to meet professionals within your field. It allows you to practice and show off your hard and soft skills in real-life settings. It is a "real" job regardless of whether your internship is paid. Students who do well in their internships and practical experiences are often offered jobs at their internship sites upon graduation if there are openings.

Impress your internship and practicum supervisors with your work ethic, professionalism, knowledge, skills, and acumen; many will offer you employment afterwards if they are in a position to. If they are not in a position to hire you outright, they will become part of your professional network and can point you to job leads with their professional contacts. Your internship supervisor or colleagues, provided you worked well with them, may also be able to help you find job leads and write you letters of recommendation or offer other support.

Mentorship Opportunities

Many colleges and programs offer mentorship opportunities with industry professionals or alumni as a value-added service for students. You should definitely take advantage of this if your program provides it. You will connect and build both your skills and network by doing this. Your mentor can provide real-life insight into the industry and put your training into perspective while sharing his or her knowledge and skills with you directly. If you cultivate a strong relationship with your mentor, he may also help you get hired at his organization or connect you to job leads with people at organizations within his professional network.

Finding Potential Companies

Regardless of whether you are fortunate enough to do an internship or practicum, you should be researching companies you'd like to work for and looking at job listings to learn which companies are hiring in your field or the area where you'll be living upon graduation. The process of researching potential companies to work for is similar to the research you did to determine which college to attend. Keep in mind that jobs are a two-way street; employers are determining whether you are a fit for the job while you are researching whether they are a good fit for you. If you are lucky enough to have multiple job offers, you have the luxury to pick and choose whom you would like to work for. Following are steps for finding the right company to work for.

Researching a Company

Make a list of potential employers you want to work for and visit their websites. If a company website is unavailable, give the company a call or pay it a visit. Some of the things you will want to be versed in so you know what you are getting into and to look competent when applying for a job include:

- **Mission:** Know the organization's mission. Ultimately, every employee hired by a company in some way contributes to achieving the organization's mission. Find out what role you would play in helping to achieve the company's mission if hired. If the company's mission is not something you can get behind, then rule out the company as a potential place to work.

- **Products and Services:** Know the products and services the company offers. As an employee, you serve as the organization's ambassador. You will impress during the application process if you know the company's products and services. Conversely, if the company offers products or services you are not comfortable supporting or passionate about, you can rule it out as a place you'd like to work.

- **Strategic Plans:** See whether you can find a copy of the organization's strategic plan if it has one or if it's publicly available. All employees perform job functions that align and support an organization's strategic plan, so review it. Then you will impress during the application process by showing you have done your homework and that you can envision yourself helping to achieve the strategic plan. Conversely, if there are aspects of the plan you cannot support, it may be an indicator that the organization is not a good fit for you.

- **Company Culture:** Company culture is a critical thing. It is one thing to be able to perform a work task; it is another to thrive in an environment. You may possess the skills to perform a job, but if the company culture cultivates an atmosphere you cannot perform in, the fit is bad. Company culture is something you need to experience by visiting the workplace or by learning about it from speaking with people who have worked at the organization. Visit the organization to assess it, talk to current or former employees, or read on the Internet what employees have posted about their experiences to get a sense of what the company culture is like.

- **How You Will Contribute:** After doing all of your research, the critical question to ask yourself is "How do I see myself contributing at this company?" Can you perform the job tasks being asked in employment postings? Do you support the company's mission? Can you help it achieve its strategic objectives? Do you stand behind the products and services it offers? Do you fit in with the company culture? Long-term or short-term, do you see yourself able to contribute to the organization's mission and objectives? What do you bring to the table for this organization? What unique things can you offer to this organization that only you can bring?

- **Network:** Build and leverage your network for any potential ins with the organizations you are considering. Do you have family members, friends, or classmates who work or have worked there? If you don't know anyone personally, does your school have any alumni who work at these organizations whom you can connect with or leverage? The old adage of "It's not what you know, but who you know" always holds true. You need to network. Network also with the employees at the organization by conducting yourself professionally with them and letting them know of your interest in becoming one of their colleagues.

- **Visit the Company and Get to Know the People:** Just as you visited your college campus to get to know it before you accepted an admissions offer there, visit a company if you are serious about being employed there one day. People have a tendency to hire people they know and are familiar with. It's a safer bet to hire a known commodity than to take a chance and bring in an outsider, unless the outsider has a strong professional record or the goal is to enhance the company gene pool with outside thoughts and ideas. Therefore, the more you visit, network, and put your name out there with the organization, the more your name will be known. If you impress enough to make a positive impression, you will have built the "in" you need to get a job offer.

Develop a LinkedIn profile

Social media is very powerful for building connections. You will want to leverage it by setting up a LinkedIn profile as soon as possible. LinkedIn is basically your online professional resume and portfolio with social networking tools to connect you to others in your industry and to job postings and leads. Continue to develop your LinkedIn profile throughout college to reflect the skills you have learned to date. Join LinkedIn groups for professionals in your field. You might also use LinkedIn to find potential internship sites and job leads after graduation.

Join Industry and Professional Associations

Every industry has one or more professional associations. Join them once you have the means so you can get your name out there. Many of these associations have junior chapters for college students or young professionals entering the field. Research what the professional associations for your profession are and find local chapters to participate in. Attend meetings, events, or conferences as your schedule and budget allow. You will make valuable contacts and learn what the issues facing your industry and profession are.

Leverage Your College Network

Your college alumni association or network, particularly if there is one for your major, will be a major resource for finding job opportunities. Given that professionals in your major often hire alumni from their alma maters, being a member of the alumni association or alumni network will provide invaluable contacts. If you belonged to an honor society, particularly a discipline-specific one, you will also be able to leverage your membership and make connections with alumni locally and around the country who may give extra preference to hiring fellow alumni who are society members. If you were a member of a sorority or fraternity, you may also have increased job opportunities and network connections from alumni in your society who look to hire or assist brothers or sisters in getting their start. One of the major benefits of belonging to honor societies or Greek organizations is leveraging the extended network for employment assistance into companies or organizations founded or primarily staffed by legacy members.

Present Yourself Well

Ultimately, when it comes to finding a job to start your career, you need to present yourself well in all forms. You need to look well on paper. You need to present yourself well in person. You need to present yourself well in your online presence. In this section, I'll talk about areas you'll want to bear in mind to present the best you.

- **Resume:** Work to prepare a professional resume summing up your skills, educational highlights, relevant work history, and any awards and recognitions you've earned. Your goal is to highlight your achievements. It's a good idea to build a "master resume" that highlights your entire background in terms of education, work history, accomplishments, professional achievements, awards earned, and skill summaries. Keep this master resume updated and on file as you continue your education and work history throughout your college experience and beyond into your job field.

- **Customize for the Specific Company:** As you begin searching for work, try to customize your resume for the specific industry or companies you are hoping to get a job with. Reframe parts of your resume to highlight your specific education or work accomplishments that hit on things the job posting is specifically looking for. You should always endeavor to customize your resume for the job you are applying for as opposed to submitting a generic resume.

- **Cover Letter:** Coupled with your resume, you should work on writing cover letters for jobs. Cover letters should always speak specifically to how you meet the requirements for the job you are applying for and how you can contribute to the organizational mission. This is where the research you've conducted into the company comes into play. A cover letter that references knowledge of what the company does, where it plans to go, and how you specifically can contribute to its mission is a much more powerful cover letter than a generic one that simply says, "I need a job and it looks like I can do the work you need done." Employers will tend to pick a candidate who has more passion for a specific company and can do the work, as opposed to a candidate who can do the work but just needs a job—any job.

Bottom line, show your prospective employer that you did your homework on the organization and the job and that you know how you specifically can contribute best. Over the years, I've sat on many job screening committees, and the cover letters that show the candidate meets the requirements and has a knowledge and understanding of the industry or the organization's challenges resulted in interviews when generic cover letters did not.

Interview Skills

Spend some time practicing your interview skills with a career counselor at your school, a career coach, or a good friend. Anticipate and write down some questions you can expect your interviewer will ask you and practice how you will answer them. Get feedback and tips from the person you are practicing with. Be able, as a bare minimum, to explain the following:

- Your educational background, training, and skills and how they allow you to meet the job requirements

- Your work history and how it allows you to meet the job requirements. If your work history is not specifically in the field you are applying for, show how the skills you have learned in your previous jobs are transferable to the job you are applying for

Review and make a list of all the job functions, requirements, and qualifications stated in the job posting. Come up with an answer for each and every requirement and qualification, highlighting how your education and experience matches each point. Find an illustrative story from your education or work history that highlights how you meet the requirement.

Work to calm your nerves by practicing your answers out loud. In the event you can't practice with a counselor, coach, or friend, simply practice in front of a mirror. Part of an interview's goal is to show your potential employer that you possess the ability to communicate effectively orally. In your work, you will need to communicate orally with colleagues, customers, or clients. Work to maintain good eye contact and smile. Part of presenting yourself well is coming across as natural and friendly. Ultimately, you need to represent yourself as competent, approachable, and professional.

Look and Behave Professionally

Dress appropriately and professionally for your interview, and behave professionally when entering the premises. You will also want to be mindful of your conduct in public settings. Never do things that reflect badly on you. You never know who may see you. The person interviewing or hiring you could very well be the person you let an elevator door shut on, or the person you cut off on the freeway or in the parking lot, or the person you bumped into on the street or at the mall without an apology.

Be Professional on Social Media

In this day and age, you also want to be aware of how you come across on social media. Many employers now check candidates' social media profiles as part of the screening process. Be mindful of what and how you post and how it can reflect on you. There have been many instances of folks not getting hired or even losing their jobs over controversial things they've posted on social media. If you plan to post controversial content that can reflect on your professional image, use your privacy settings to bury that type of content to your most trusted followers.

Take Advantage of Campus Career Services

Most colleges and universities provide career service offices that filter job listings from employers and help you develop your resume, cover letter, and interview skills. These services are typically free. Take advantage of these services in your job search.

SUMMARY

We all enter school with the ultimate goal of developing our skills to find a job and start a career. As you go through school, keep your eye on the prize, and take steps to build your skills and professional network to help find your post-college job while still a student. Some things you can do include:

- Impress your professors to earn a good recommendation letter and leverage their networks.

- Participate in an internship or practicum, and impress your supervisors and colleagues enough to earn a job offer or a strong recommendation to employment opportunities with their professional contacts.

- Start building your professional network while a student by joining professional, trade, and industry associations, or online networking groups or social sites such as LinkedIn.

- Connect with your high school and college alumni network to leverage and find job leads and expand your network.

- Treat finding a job with the right company the same way you found the right school; do your homework and research.

- Know the mission, products, and services of the companies you wish to work for and see how you fit in with the companies. You're interviewing the company just as much as it is interviewing you.

- Build a master resume.

- Customize your resume and cover letter specifically for each job you apply for, based on your research into the organization. State how you can help the organization achieve its mission based on your unique skills and background.

- Practice your job interview skills.

- Conduct yourself as a professional at all times in public and on social media.
- Use your school's career services center.

"Nothing in the world can take the place of persistence. Talent will not; nothing is more common than unsuccessful men with talent. Genius will not; unrewarded genius is almost a proverb. Education will not; the world is full of educated derelicts. Persistence and determination alone are omnipotent. The slogan "press on" has solved and will always solve the problems of the human race."

— Calvin Coolidge

YOUR COLLEGE AND LIFE ROADMAP

We all enter college with the goal of getting a good paying job in our career field after graduation. Part of your college and life success plan is to think ahead and lay the groundwork for launching your career as quickly as possible after graduation. All of this groundwork should be laid during your time as a student. Let's start putting together your career launch plan!

Exercise 1: Internships or Practicum Experiences

Find out whether your program requires or offers an optional internship or practicum experience. If it does, start thinking about potential organizations you can have your experience with.

Exercise 2: Research Your Preferred Companies

Which organizations would you like to work for? Build a list of twenty potential organizations and start to research their missions, products and services, strategic plans, and company cultures. Do you have contacts or potential contacts who work there?

Exercise 3: Mentorship Programs

Does your college or program offer a mentorship program with professionals in your field? If it doesn't, informally inquire with a professor or counselor whether he or she would be able to connect you with a potential mentor.

Exercise 4: Professional Associations

What professional organizations or associations are there in your industry? Which ones would you like to join?

Exercise 5: Alumni Associations

Find out whether your high school, college, or program has an alumni association that does professional mixers or directory listings for career networking purposes. Associations may maintain websites or email lists that send out job postings. Bookmark these pages or subscribe to these lists.

Exercise 6: Privileged Networks

If you are a member of an honor society, sorority, or fraternity, start to network and see what types of career or job leads you can discover by connecting with alumni members. National chapters, regional chapters, and local chapters often maintain a job posting system or email lists that send out job leads to alumni. Bookmark these sites or subscribe to these lists.

Exercise 7: LinkedIn

Create a profile on LinkedIn and join industry or trade groups on LinkedIn.

Exercise 8: Craft Your Resume

Start to develop your master resume.

Exercise 9: Career Center or Services Office

Find the career services office at your school and meet the staff or attend workshops or info sessions it may offer.

A Final Word

ACHIEVING YOUR DESTINY

> "There is no end to education. It is not that you read a book, pass an examination, and finish with education. The whole of life, from the moment you are born to the moment you die, is a process of learning."
>
> — Jiddu Krishnamurti

Congratulations on finishing this book! Now that you've finished reading *Succeeding in College and Life*, what do you plan to do next? If you've read through this book and completed the exercises, you will have the tools and skills you need to succeed in college and, with time and practice, life. With all of that said, what will you do next to start or advance your college career? If you're re-reading this book as you near graduation, what will you do next to move your career forward? What goals will you set for yourself? What specific steps will you take next to move forward in accomplishing your dreams?

I challenge you to take action today because the early bird always catches the worm. Throughout this book, I've equipped you with all the tools you need to be a successful college student. I want to see you succeed, so I challenge you now to start taking the steps needed to get into the school of your choice, to find the career direction you need to pick a good major, and to apply for the funding you need to minimize your debt or the financial burden you and your family will undertake.

As a first step, use the lines below to determine the first ten action steps you will take over the next ninety days to move forward with setting yourself up for college success.

1. _____
   _____

2. _____
   _____

3. _____
   _____

4. _____
   _____

5. _____
   _____

6. _____
   _____

7. _____
   _____

8. _____
   _____

9. _____
   _____

10. _____
    _____

Over the course of this book, you've prepared for college success! You've set career goals. You've found the right schools for you. You've learned how to fund your college education. You've learned the various skills you'll need to survive your college years, including taking notes, studying for exams, managing your time, managing your money, writing papers, reading books, and conducting research. You've been coached on how to develop your mental, spiritual, and emotional fortitude to help carry you through the stresses and tough times that will emerge during your college years. Finally, you've discovered the secrets for jumpstarting your career and developing your professional network to lead to career opportunities upon graduation.

Now that you've read my book, I encourage you to contact me and tell me what you liked or disliked about it so I can improve it for the next printing. More importantly, I'd love to hear about you and your challenges so I can be part of your support team in succeeding in college and in life! I invite you to schedule a thirty-minute, no obligation consultation by phone, Skype, Google Hangout, FaceTime, or (if geographically possible) face-to-face meeting to learn how I can assist you more in achieving your dreams!

My email address is askcoachjon@gmail.com and my cell number is (646)-481-5198. Please email or text me with your name and time zone and I'll be glad to schedule your complimentary consultation.

Wherever you are in life, whether you're just starting your college journey straight out of high school or are returning to school to retrain yourself or start a new career, I wish you the best of luck and send my blessings. I thank you for allowing me to be a part of your journey.

> "If you don't go after what you want, you'll never have it.
> If you don't ask, the answer is always no.
> If you don't step forward, you're always in the same place."
>
> — Nora Roberts

To your college and life success!

With aloha, your friend,

Jonathan K Wong

Jonathan Wong
Honolulu, Hawaii

ABOUT THE AUTHOR

Jonathan K. Wong, MBA, M.Ed., MPA is a Honolulu-born and based author, blogger, podcaster, professional speaker, success coach, and organizational consultant. A former college instructor, counselor, technology trainer, instructional designer, and administrative professional of fifteen years alongside being a trained and certified Information Technology professional, Jonathan now travels the road teaching success seminars and workshops and delivering keynotes on topics such as academic success and career, business, and leadership development. A Native-Hawaiian professional, he takes special interest in working with indigenous and minority-serving clients and organizations.

Throughout his academic career, Jonathan earned his advanced degrees in business administration, education technology, and public administration, and over the years, he has lent his expertise in technology and business to various individuals and organizations through his Akamai Visionary Consulting practice.

Jonathan's hobbies include studying the martial arts; learning about alternative, traditional, and complementary healing styles; playing video games; and watching superhero movies and professional wrestling. He has extensive studies in Chinese kung fu in the Hung Gar and Choy Li Fut styles, Okinawan Karate in the Shorin-Ryu and Uechi Ryu styles, Muay Thai boxing, Brazilian Jiu-Jitsu, and the ancient Hawaiian martial art of Lua. In his alternative and complementary healing studies, he has done extensive study as an energy healer and bodyworker, having certified as a Reiki Master (Uesui style) and Pranic Healer, and has studied bodywork modalities, including Thai Massage, Reflexology, Cranial Sacral Therapy, and Hawaiian Lomilomi.

A part-time performance artist, Jonathan is trained in

improvisational theatre and as a TV, film, and voice actor. He performed for several years with several Honolulu-based troupes and theatre companies in short form and long form improv. As an actor, he occasionally performs supporting roles in various independent films and web productions, and he provides voice work for various projects.

He is always available for success coaching, organizational consulting, trainings, seminars, workshops, and keynote speaking gigs.

Jonathan resides in Honolulu with his fiancée Liane.

PONO LIFE COACHING

Create the life of your dreams with the guidance and accountability of an experienced success coach! Jonathan Wong, MBA, M.Ed, MPA, is a success coach specializing in the areas of academics, career, business, and leadership. A college instructor and counselor of fifteen years, he has worked with thousands of students to help them succeed in their studies, transition into their careers, and develop the leadership skills they need to succeed in life. A small business owner himself, Jonathan holds a graduate business degree, and he has also coached hundreds and helped them to launch their businesses.

Through his Pono Life Coaching practice, Jonathan will help you or your loved ones to get ahead in life while maintaining your life balance. Whether you're looking for guidance through your studies, are ready to launch your career or your small business, or are looking to take your leadership skills to the next level, Jonathan Wong and Pono Life Coaching will be there to support you 1000 percent (not a typo!) of the way.

Group Coaching and One-On-One Coaching plans are available. Packages are available in six-month, one-year, multi-year, and lifetime combinations. Family discounts are available as well.

ponolifecoaching.com
askcoachjon@gmail.com
call/text: (646) 481-5198

AKAMAI VISIONARY CONSULTING

Consulting * Reorganizations * Strategic Planning * Software Solutions * Training and Development

With graduate degrees in Business Administration, Educational Technology, and Public Administration, Jonathan Wong works with schools and colleges to unlock their potential and guide them to success. Having started his career in Information Technology and Information Systems before transitioning to work in advising and teaching, Jonathan has the unique skills and capabilities to guide institutions at a high level through transitory times. Available for consulting work, conducting institutional studies, developing strategic or tactical plans, and conducting faculty or staff development workshops or seminars, Jonathan will love bringing out the best in your institution and helping you fulfill your potential. Whether you are implementing a new IT system, undergoing a campus reorganization or conducting an institutional review and study, Jonathan offers his considerable skills, drawing upon his studies in business, education, public administration, and information technology, and he couples those with his understanding of the needs of instructional, academic support, and student services staff and units to develop solutions that work To find out how Jonathan can help you or your organization, contact him at:

akamaivisionary.com
call/text: (646) 481-5198
jon@akamaivisionary.com

JONATHAN SPEAKS

Entertain * Educate * Engage

As a gifted and prolific speaker and entertainer, Jonathan Wong draws on his years of studies, teaching experience, and performance background to craft a unique presentation for your audience.

An instructor and trainer of fifteen years with expertise in leadership, academic success skills, business, health and wellness, life balance, and goal setting, Jonathan speaks on various topics of interest to academic audiences.

A performing artist of over a decade, Jonathan is a trained actor, comedian, and musician, having performed on Honolulu's improv, sketch, stand-up comedy, and independent film scene for over ten years. Raised in a musical family and having gone on to elective music studies at the high school and college level, today Jonathan is a vocalist, guitarist, and ukulele musician who covers genres ranging from inspirational music to acoustic contemporary. His speaking engagements always hit the mark in terms of educating the audience on the topic while providing an entertaining and engaging experience that incorporates a unique combination of comedic and musical entertainment.

Hire Jonathan today for any of the following:

- School Assemblies
- New Student Orientations
- Honor Society Induction Ceremonies
- Career Fair Keynotes
- Business Fair Keynotes
- Health Fair Keynotes
- Convocations
- Commencement Ceremonies

SPEAKING TOPICS INCLUDE:

- Visioning: Life's Mission and Goal Setting
- Developing Your Inner Leader
- All-Star Teamwork for College and Beyond
- The College Entrepreneur
- How to Launch Your Career While Still in School
- Leading a Balanced Life When It All Needs to Be Done
- Overcoming Depression and Other Mental Illnesses
- Bouncing Back from Failures and Setbacks
- Money Management for the College Student
- Resetting and Rebuilding Your Life as a Non-Traditional Student
- Avoiding Alcohol or Drug Addiction
- Sexual Assault Isn't Cool

To discuss with Jonathan how he can wow your audience and leave it wanting more, contact him at:

jonathanwongspeaks.com
call/text: (213) 262-9570
jonathanwong.bookings@gmail.com

DRIVE FOR UBER OR LYFT

Need extra money for books, tuition, or living expenses? Take advantage of the flexible income opportunities offered by rideshare driving for Uber or Lyft! If you're twenty-one or older, have a clean driving and criminal record, and have access to a qualifying car, you can make money driving people as an Uber or Lyft driver partner! Some of the benefits of being a rideshare driver include:

- You are your own boss! No one to answer to. No performance reviews.
- Drive around *your* schedule. No shifts to keep. No reporting time. No ending time. Drive whenever you like.
- Get paid weekly or even daily! Yes, daily!
- Meet people from all over!

Drive for *both* Uber and Lyft! Double the opportunity to make money Sign up bonuses are available depending on your city upon meeting the minimum number of ride requirements. Promotions vary by city. Visit the Uber or Lyft websites or download the apps from the Apple or Google Play stores, and sign up today with the following referral codes to be eligible to earn sign-up rewards:

Uber Referral Code: 7avf4qscue

Lyft Referral Code: JONATHAN008938

Learn how to maximize your driver earnings by also reading Jonathan Wong's book *Driving Profits and Making Bank* to learn the rideshare game and leverage your driving gig into additional opportunities.